A FIELD ATLAS
OF THE SEASHORE

Julian Cremona

St Mary's College, Southampton

ACKNOWLEDGEMENTS

I would like to thank Tony Hogg for reading the manuscript and giving much helpful criticism. In my early days of running field courses, Alec Cooper was always full of useful comments, some of which are incorporated here and I owe much to the Allnatt Fieldcentre, The Chatsworth, in Swanage, England. Discussions with Deenea Wright and Andrew Fleming at the centre invariably entered the early hours! My thanks to Geoff Cooper for helping with the photographs and to Bob Henry of Cartographical Services (Southampton) Ltd. for the aerial views of salt-marsh and estuary.

Perhaps some of the greatest inspiration has been from my many students over the years but always it has been my wife, Brenda, that has given me the most encouragement and patience.

Cover photo from Heather Angel/Biophotos

Published by the Press Syndicate of the University of Cambridge
The Pitt Building, Trumpington Street, Cambridge CB2 1RP
40 West 20th Street, New York, NY 10011–4211, USA
10 Stamford Road, Oakleigh, Melbourne 3166, Australia

First published 1988
Third printing 1995

Printed in Malta by Interprint Limited

British Library cataloguing in publication data

Cremona, Julian
   A field atlas of the seashore.
   1. Seashore biology – Great Britain
   I. Title
   574.941   QH95.7

ISBN 0 521 34799 8

VN

CONTENTS

PREFACE

A greater awareness of our environment has been encouraged for some years by examination boards and teachers. With the advent of GCSE and the changing 'A' level syllabuses there is a need to look again at our approach to ecological studies. Studying the interrelationships of animals and plants with their environment makes us pose a number of questions about an organism:

What is it?

What is its name?

What type of organism is it?

What are the limitations and adaptations of this organism?

Where does it live?

What factors limit the distribution of the organism?

How do these factors work?

How does it live there?

The prospects are daunting to students when arriving at the study site to be confronted by a barrage of different species and physical or chemical features to sort out. This book helps the student to unravel these problems. Identification of species by using keys is a necessary skill that should be learnt in the course of fieldwork. However, with the wealth of life in the environment it is a very time-consuming task that easily distracts from the real feature of ecology, i.e. to understand how an ecosystem works. At the end of the hints for answering the problems, a bibliography outlines some of the main sources of keys to identification, as it is beyond the capacity of this book.

To understand the workings of the seashore it is unnecessary to identify every species and, in fact, it is really the community that should be identified rather than the individual. This book helps to identify the common organisms that are likely to be encountered around the shores of northern Europe, identify the community to which they may belong, and to explain the interaction between them and other organisms.

Before going to the study site the student should read and understand chapter one which summarises what ecology and ecosystems are all about. A brief outline of studying the seashore is also given. In addition, the introduction to each chapter of the chosen ecosystem should be read. The ecosystem is then dealt with by communities.

Opposite a photograph of each community the limiting factors and features for that community are stated followed by the adaptations of the indigenous organisms to those problems. It may then be followed by further details of the biology of those organisms.

At times it has been necessary to simplify relationships for a book of this size and scope. Details are often abbreviated to give as much information on the relevant pages as possible.

The second part of each chapter deals with explaining the relationships between the organisms and the communities. It is expected that this will help in the conclusions and discussion of the work back in the laboratory. Finally, a set of ecological problems are given, based on projects that could be done by students, which test some of the concepts. A short glossary is at the back. However, there is no substitute for getting nipped by a crab or leaving your welly behind in the mud!

Julian Cremona
Southampton, 1987

WHAT IS ECOLOGY?

THE BASIC PRINCIPLES

Ecology is concerned with the relationship between living things and their external environment. Animals also have an internal environment consisting of tissue fluid which bathes the body cells. Higher organisms, e.g. mammals, can regulate this fluid (**homeostasis**) within narrow limits but moving down the phyla series to lower invertebrates there is a progressive lessening of control and a greater dependence on the conditions within the external environment. For example, sea anemones have no control over water loss or the water entering their tissue fluid. They must live in an aquatic environment where the concentration (osmotic potential) matches that of their tissue fluid so that water loss will equal water gain. As well as water they must obtain glucose, protein, salts and oxygen from the environment. Here we see the fundamental relationship between an organism and its environment. Each organism has its specific needs for survival and to understand an organism it is important to understand its external environment.

THE ECOSYSTEM

No organism is independent. We are all part of an ecological system. The seashore as an environment is made up of a number of such ecosystems. An ecosystem is not a tangible item but a theoretical relationship between four interacting components:

1. the **biota** – the communities of animals and plants
2. the **abiota** – the physical and chemical features determining the system
3. an **energy source**, e.g. solar energy which powers a system through photosynthesis
4. a **flow of nutrients** – the cycle of decomposition, e.g. nitrogen and carbon cycles.

The abiota are the factors which form the limitations of the ecosystem and will determine the presence and development of an organism. These may be termed **limiting factors**. They define the environment of the organism and fluctuation causing **environmental stress** may result in the death of the organism. Ecosystems will have several primary limiting factors which may in turn control secondary ones. On the seashore, tides and wave action are the primary factors affecting oxygenation and substrate (secondary limiting factors).

THE SEASHORE AND WAVE ACTION

The shoreline or **littoral** region is the area between high and low water marks. Its formation is an interaction of waves and geology. Waves determine the coastline. A wave is a wind-induced oscillation of the water surface, its energy continues until expended or deflected by an object. Two wave types can be identified: the pounding wave (an eroding wave) and the spilling wave (a depositing wave).

Eroding wave: the full force of the wave is striking the shore; deep water is just offshore

Depositing wave: offshore it is shallow and the underside of the wave causes it to spill over; by the time the waves reach the shore all the energy is spent and any suspended material present will drop to the bottom

TYPES OF SEASHORE

Wave action determines the substrate on the shore and therefore the type of shore which will develop. Eroding waves scour the land revealing rocky shores; depositing waves produce a build up of shingle or sand. As wave action stops altogether muddy shores develop.

THE TIDES

Twice a day the water rises and falls across the littoral region. These tides are of two types: **neap tides** and **spring tides**. The latter has nothing to do with the seasons but has a greater rise and fall than a neap tide. The extent of this **tidal range** will vary from place to place and from day to day. Dorset in England has a range of 1–2 metres; the Channel Islands has a range of 5–10 metres. The tidal range varies on a monthly cycle, with a week of neap tides followed by a week of spring tides. During the neaps (which coincide with the first and second quarters of the moon) there appears to be little movement: the lower shore never uncovering and the upper shore receiving little or no water. Spring tides coincide with new and full moons and uncover the lower shore and wet the upper shore twice a day. The extent changes gradually through the week as it comes into neaps and vice versa. An organism living on the upper shore only receives seawater for a short time every other week. On the lower shore uncovering occurs for a short time, once a fortnight. In this way there is a gradient of limiting factors across the habitat. The abiota relevant to each type of shore is given under the respective chapter.

COMMUNITIES

Populations of animals and plants interact within a **community**. Usually, there is a dominant species which we recognise as an **indicator** of the environmental conditions. Marram grass gives its name to the marram community typical of wind-blown sand. A number of communities may live within an ecosystem. It is not a random mix of species but an orderly distribution of communities changing along the gradient of limiting factors. As the conditions change so the community merges with another. This produces bands of communities: **zonation**. On the rocky shore there is a static zonation, unchanged spatially from year to year. Dynamic zonation is typical of the plants of sand dunes and salt-marsh where a succession of communities replace each other in time: **ecological succession**.

Spiral wrack at low tide: after 30 minutes exposure

Spiral wrack at low tide: after 8 hours exposure

THE ECOLOGICAL NICHE

Many people have tried to explain the term niche, which is attributed to each species. The simplest definition is its place of residence, but this is grossly inadequate. The edges of the niche will be defined by the upper and lower boundary of limiting factors. Here we can consider the two: tides (exposing to desiccation) and wave action. Start by drawing a box, the sides of which represent a gradient of that factor from none to the maximum. Somewhere along each line the species can live. See Fig. 1. A1 to A2 are the points of desiccation between which our species can tolerate; B1 to B2 are the limits of tolerance to wave action. At the corners of the box, where the factors interact it is lethal and so we draw a circle within the box to represent the **potential niche** of the organism. Within this circle the organism can live, outside it is lethal. The nearer the centre, the less environmental stress there will be as the conditions are optimal there: the **op-**

timum niche. This diagram was coined the '*n*-dimensional fried egg' by Dowdeswell and Sinker. The number of dimensions of the box vary according to the number of primary limiting factors. Every niche will have a 'bite' taken out of it and this may be where it is overlapping with another species whose demands on the environment are similar – this is **competition**. In each chapter there will be examples of overlapping niches, e.g. bladder-wrack and knotted wrack. They both occupy the same A1 to A2 in coping with desiccation. They differ in wave action tolerance where the former has a wide range and, in theory, would dominate the latter. However, knotted wrack always shades out the other and so takes a large chunk out of its 'fried egg'. A second reason for the space is **predation**. A rocky shore dominated by limpets will graze the rock surface clear of any seaweed sporelings. Bladder-wrack never gets the chance to develop and another bite has been removed from its niche. Barnacle distribution down the shore is stopped by dog-whelks which feed on them. The end result of the bites taken out of our 'fried egg' is termed the **realised niche**.

PRIMARY PRODUCTION

This is the assimilation of energy and nutrients by photo- and chemosynthesis. **Producers** are organisms capable of fixing the energy within the ecosystem, e.g. the algae of the rocky shore. The energy available for assimilation on the seashore is not constant throughout and is a contributory factor to zonation. Primary production is greatest at the lower shore levels where there is greater diversity and biomass of algae. It declines towards the upper shore where there are a few species of lichen at the top. But primary production is also influenced by environmental conditions, increased wave action causes a drastic reduction in production. It is also important to remember that the diatoms in the **phytoplankton** constitute an important source of primary production.

The producers are ingested by herbivorous **consumers** which may themselves be consumed by carnivorous consumers, thus forming a chain or **food web**. The energy which passes through the web of organisms follows a pathway through energy levels called **trophic** levels, autotrophs consumed by heterotrophs.

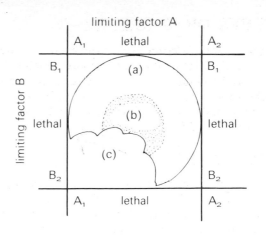

(a) potential niche
(b) optimal niche
(c) competition and predation with other organisms

Fig. 1 The **realised niche** as shown by the '*n*'-dimensional fried egg (after Dowdeswell and Sinker 1977)

PYRAMID OF NUMBERS

If an area of shoreline is marked out and the numbers of organisms present in each trophic level counted they can be plotted as a pyramid, such that the width of each band in the pyramid is a measure of their density (Fig. 2a). Each successive layer in the food web must be smaller than the one before as the transfer of energy is very small, most is lost as heat, faeces and urine. The more balanced the ecosystem, the wider the base. In the pyramid of numbers the differences between trophic levels are not well marked. Consider the animals living on one seaweed, e.g. the sea oak, they greatly outnumber the single plant (Fig. 2b) and a pyramid of parasites will be inverted – one host, tens of parasites and each parasite with hundreds of hyperparasites (Fig. 2c).

A **pyramid of biomass** takes this all into consideration and produces a more balanced picture of an ecosystem. But even here there are a few anomalies. When the oyster-catcher eats a mussel it leaves the shell which, although it is protein, is indigestible. Biomass would include the shell, hence the ultimate measurement of energy in the ecosystem would be a **pyramid of energy**, where a calorimeter could be used to measure the energy value of the food consumed in joules per gram.

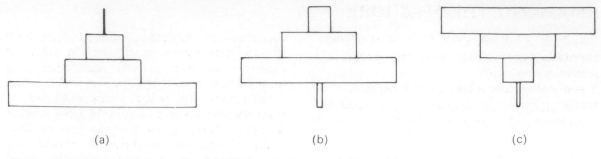

Fig. 2 Pyramid of numbers for the middle shore (a), for sea oak (b), and for parasitic communities (c)

DECOMPOSITION AND NUTRIENT FLOW

One of the components of the ecosystem is the flow of nutrients. In the estuary, as well as organic material being present from the salt-marsh plants it washes downstream from the freshwater ecosystem, the tides bring in dead material from the sea. Organisms in the community called **decomposers**, such as bacteria and protozoans, then break down the organic matter in such a way that soluble substances escape into the water. Tidal movements may flush much of the nutrient away. This flow of essential nutrients between ecosystems can be quite balanced. For example, a cow may fall over the cliff and die, so adding nutrients to the seashore whilst land birds often feed on the upper shore in winter taking nutrients back to the land.

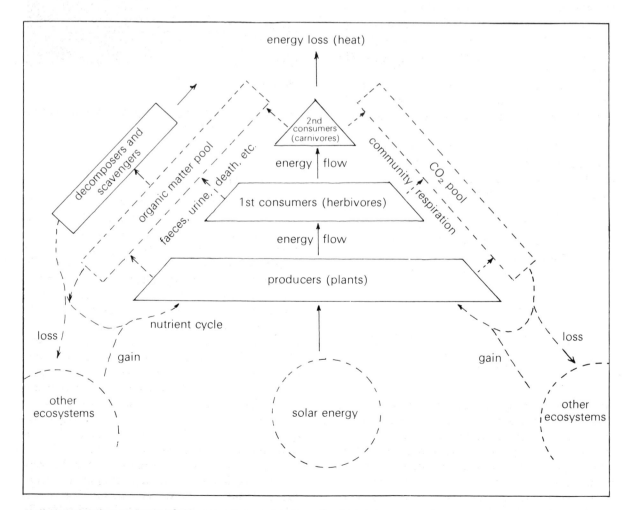

A diagrammatic summary of the ecosystem and energy flow

STUDYING THE SEASHORE

Fieldwork can be divided into two areas of study:

* **autecology** the study of an individual species and
* **synecology** the study of communities.

When studying the seashore both should be considered and compared.

AUTECOLOGY

A population of organisms has a number of properties such as population density, a birth and death rate, growth form and reproductive fitness. To study even a few of these requires time and patience. Density and growth form are particularly important and studying them can give reasonable results over several days. Choice of species is important and molluscs give good results with this type of work. The technique given below is for the rough periwinkle but could be adapted for many seashore animals.

A sample plot needs to be marked out on the rocks; a square with 4 m sides can have the corners marked with a blob of paint. The area should then be searched and a sample of periwinkles removed (about 200). These individuals are now marked so they can be recognised again. A small spot of enamel paint, such as 'Humbrol', can be applied to the top of the shell. The height of the shell is also measured and can be plotted as a frequency histogram to see the growth form of the population. The periwinkles are carefully placed back into their habitat where they were before.

The following day, after the tides have washed over them, the plot is again sampled with individuals removed at random. The numbers of marked and unmarked specimens is recorded and from the formula below the population density calculated. The statistical theory behind this is that if the density was 1000 and you marked 200, then upon recapturing a sample the ratio of marked to unmarked should be about 1:5.

$$\text{Population density} = \frac{P \times N}{n}$$

Where P = number marked on the first day

N = total number recaptured, marked and unmarked

n = number recaptured marked

When considering the results of this investigation it is important to consider possible errors. Valid results depend on the marked ones becoming part of the population once more as if nothing had happened. Bright paint will attract attention from predators and also affect the way you recapture them, biasing the result. For some species painting like this could spoil its chances at courtship, an important factor in long term studies. Paint is an unsuitable marking technique for arthropods over a period of time. Why? Long term work can yield information on birth and death rates as the density changes. Groups of students should select plots in different areas of the upper shore, e.g. creviced and non-creviced, rock pools, and compare the density results. The density can be related to availability of food and predation. Painting individuals for recognition is useful so that they can be tracked from a common release point and a measurement of the distances travelled can be analysed.

Marking and measuring rough periwinkles in the mark and recapture technique

SYNECOLOGY

The abiota produce a gradient of stress across the ecosystem which in turn affects the distribution of communities. To study this a **transect** is used. Basically, this is a series of samples taken at set intervals along a line across the ecosystem. The length of the line and the intervals will depend on the extent of the shore. If the area to be studied is very extensive, e.g. a sand dunes system, then the samples should be replaced by sampling stations and at each station 5–10 random samples taken. The sampling could be done by recording species touching the line but a **quadrat** is the most accurate method. This is usually a square frame which forms a fixed area in which to search for organisms. Choosing the size of the frame requires careful consideration to ensure that the sample is representative for the site.

The presence of an organism can be represented by a line drawn on graph paper to show the distribution. However, some idea of the relative percentage abundance is preferable. By comparing a sheltered and exposed shore by line only barnacles will show a similar pattern, but a $\%$ will depict dominance in the latter with a small number present in the former. The sampling station idea can yield large numbers of presence and absence which easily convert to a percentage. In Fig. 3, 50 random quadrat throws were made at each station on the dune. Marram in station 1 appeared 14 times (28% of sample). These figures can then be plotted as a histogram or a kite diagram. On the rocky shore where fewer samples may be taken, it is easier to divide the quadrat frame into a grid, record the number of times the organism occurs in each grid and convert to a percentage.

Over very short distances, e.g. 6 m in the upper salt-marsh, a belt transect records the presence of dominant species by drawing a scale map of distribution between two lines one metre apart.

A **profile transect** takes into account the slope of the shore. One of the easiest ways of doing this is to fill a 5 m length of clear plastic tubing with water, leaving an air space at either end (as shown in the picture below). Hold both ends against metre rules which are held vertically. The levels of water in the tube will always stay the same. Place the rules at a set interval apart, e.g. 2 metres, the height of the water level is noted at each end and the difference is the change in height of the slope over that distance. This should be carried out with the line transect.

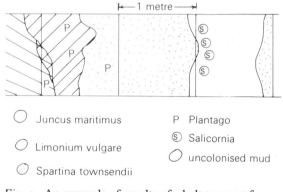

Fig. 3 An example of part of the results of a sand dune transect

Fig. 4 An example of results of a belt transect from a salt-marsh

Students on a rocky shore: in the foreground they are measuring % algal growth and in the background they are measuring the slope for the transect

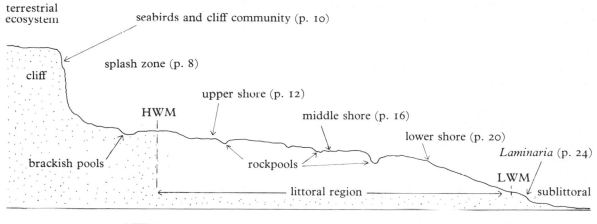

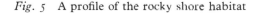

HWM – high water mark   LWM – low water mark

Fig. 5   A profile of the rocky shore habitat

THE SUBSTRATE

This type of shore consists of eroding rock surfaces, erosion exposes them to colonisation by algae

- soft rocks may have animals which have burrowed into them whilst hard rocks are easier for algae to attach
- the angle at which the rock strata lie will affect the shore: upright strata may produce deep gullies and long rockpools; flat strata produces platforms of rock with broader, shallower rockpools
- sheltered areas of the shore will have small deposits of sand which will encourage colonisation by animals more typical of depositing shores, e.g. lugworm and *Sabellaria*
- boulders and large stones will increase the shelter afforded to animals resulting in a greater diversity of life

PROBLEMS AND FEATURES OF LIVING HERE

- attachment to the rock: for rooted, vascular plants this is impossible and so colonisation of the rock is dominated by algae
- obtaining nutrients: the algae obtain their minerals and other essential nutrients from the seawater
- wave action: this has a modifying influence, if

severe it will limit the communities able to survive and individual species may show variable growth, e.g. bladder-wrack and limpets
- light for photosynthesis: when the tide is out the rate of photosynthesis slows in exposed algae (why?); when the tide is in the light is filtered by the seawater so that only some wavelengths pass through

POINTS OF SPECIAL INTEREST

- zonation of the communities is clearly defined
- many taxonomic groups of animals are represented on the seashore; some groups are only found here whilst others, like the insects, have only a few species present
- algae tend to be the major producers of energy and there is a diverse range of species to be found

PRECAUTIONS IN FIELDWORK

The seaweeds are slippery but wet, seemingly bare rock can be worse because of slimy blue-green algae. Beware of falling rocks on eroding cliffs. On the lower shore of wave-exposed shores sudden wave action easily dislodges students: rope up if necessary (refer to your teacher).

SPLASH ZONE COMMUNITY

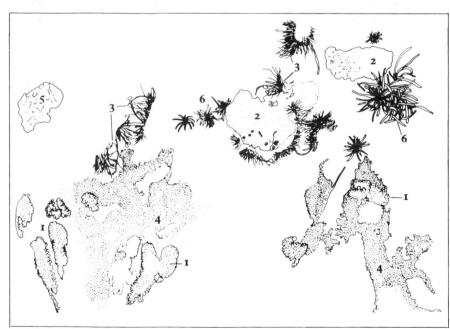

1 *Xanthoria parietina*

2 *Lecanora atra*

3 *Ramalina siliquosa*

4 *Verrucaria maura*

5 *Ochrolechia parella*

6 *Armeria maritima* (thrift)

- high salt content from spray
- extremes of temperature, desiccating wind
- very little water available
- on strandline the dumping of dead organic matter has a shading effect despite acting as a nutrient source
- uric acid (guano) from seabirds, deposited on rocks, has a 'burning' effect on vegetation

ORANGE LICHENS

Xanthoria parietina
- a leaf-like lichen with raised orange fruiting bodies in centre
- orange pigment (parietin) is present in the upper surface to protect lower algal cells from extreme sunlight, it is therefore pale on north-facing or shaded slopes
- it releases spores throughout the year
- 7% of cells are algal cells

Caloplaca marina
- encrusting lichen with knobbly surface

GREY LICHENS

Ochrolechia parella
- encrusting form with raised grey fruiting body

Lecanora atra
- encrusting form with black fruiting bodies

GREEN, FRUTICOSE LICHEN

Ramalina siliquosa
- brittle, strap-like projections of grey-green colour

BLACK ENCRUSTING LICHEN

Verrucaria maura

(see p. 13)

Armeria maritima (thrift or sea-pink)
- the probing roots are able to penetrate crevices for water and give stability
- survives in a minimum of soil, e.g. in the humus of dead lichen
- the narrow leaves reduce the surface area to slow down water loss

SUCCESSION IN THE SPLASH ZONE

Lichens are the first colonisers of bare rock. Lichens are slow growing but long-lived. As they grow the action of acids and expansion of their cells cause a slow break up of the rock into tiny fragments to produce a raw soil. This may then be colonised by mosses and, as the humus collects in crevices, by flowering plants able to tolerate the high salt content, e.g. thrift. This mini-succession is called a **lithosere** and can be found on mountain rocks. In this zone it rarely passes the flowering plant stage.

- erosion and instability, these may be increased by the presence of sea-birds
- high salt content in the soil
- high uric acid content from the sea-birds droppings
- the shallow soil will be leached, the minerals staining the cliff rock
- grazing by rabbits at the top
- strong, desiccating wind action

CLIFFS AND SEA-BIRD COLONIES

Sea-birds are the top carnivores of the coastal ecosystem. Most nest in colonies on inaccessible cliff faces, safe from mammal predators, e.g. foxes. Each species of sea-bird has its own distinct nesting behaviour and location on the cliff. This helps to avoid interspecific competition for space. The diagram below shows a possible zonation of sea-birds down a cliff but the actual arrangement depends on the availability of nesting niches, e.g. ledges or grassy slopes. Soft rocks will crumble and are unsuitable nesting sites.

The stability will depend very much on the extent of the slope. But invariably there is intense grazing at the top of the cliff by rabbits which allows only closely cropped grasses such as fescue to grow. Thrift and plantains are rabbit 'resistant', sea-beet and samphire are not, but they do have a high tolerance of salt. The community living here is a very specialised one, particularly with the high level of certain minerals from salt, uric acid and leached minerals. Sea-campion cannot tolerate grazing but is prolific around guano-covered cliff. Wind will stunt growth and increase the problem of transpiration.

Herring gull
- nests on flattish ground
- diet is varied, including chicks of other gulls
- strongly territorial

Guillemot
- nests on bare cliff ledges
- the egg has a pointed end so it rolls in circles and not over the edge
- panicked easily by gulls or man (possible predators)

Fulmar
- nests singly on ledges
- breeds when 8 years old, lives 25 yrs
- not a gull but a petrel
- feeds on offal (scavenger)

Kittiwake
- the only cliff nesting gull

Shag and cormorant
- large nests of twigs and seaweed
- able to catch large fish, no waterproofing so they spend long periods drying wings

A cliff profile showing nesting positions of the sea-birds

SPECIES OF THE SPLASH ZONE AND CLIFF

PLANTS

Lichens

Made up from two organisms, a fungus and an alga, which form a symbiotic relationship. Separately, they would require moist, sheltered conditions, together they survive a very hostile place. The fungus can store up to 35 times its weight in water. The alga is the smaller component ($< 10\%$). They grow particularly well where there is a high nitrogen content, e.g. from sea-bird droppings. *Xanthoria* may be prolific for this reason; it releases spores continually during the year. Spores consist of an algal cell encased in strands of the fungus. The orange and grey lichens in this zone are slow growing and therefore intolerant of grazing by marine snails. *Verrucaria*, found further down the shore is faster growing and hence more resistant to grazing. These salt-tolerant lichens form an important community between the tidal zone and the cliff-top flowering plants, both areas of intense grazing. The lichens are very susceptible to pollution and can be used to monitor sulphur dioxide in the air. Splash zone lichens are killed by oil pollution and some of the detergents used to disperse spillages.

Flowering plants

The plants surviving here depend on their ability to cope with the salt and desiccation, coupled with the almost total lack of soil. Thrift deals with all of this and grazing. Sea-plantain grows here and, like thrift, can survive extreme conditions; both are members of tundra communities. To avoid water loss, leaves of these plants may be narrow and succulent. This will reduce the surface area. Around the stomata of the leaves may be a dense cover of hairs, helping to retain moisture.

Prasiola stipitata

Very small, flattened green alga; approximately 1 cm² in area
- where water collects in crevices with bird guano, this green 'slime' develops
- tolerant of freshwater and water with a high salt content

See also *Enteromorpha* and *Verrucaria*.

ANIMALS

Littorina neritoides

the black periwinkle; up to 6 mm in length
- it grazes on encrusting lichens and microscopic algae
- it is tolerant of extreme temperatures, e.g. 46°C, with low metabolic rate
- it lives in crevices and the female sheds egg capsules only at high spring tides during autumn and winter when the sea is roughest
- the larva lives with plankton and when metamorphosis occurs, settles in the barnacle zone; using responses to light and gravity it migrates up to the splash zone
- it excretes uric acid which helps prevent water loss
- it is tolerant of highly variable salinity
- it possesses a lung (a modified gill cavity with capillaries)

Strandline insects

Very few insects have adapted to life on the seashore. Small white maggots are common in seaweed cast up onto the strandline. They may be from a variety of flies adapted to the salty food. *Strigamia maritima* is a centipede often seen in the splash zone feeding on the insects.

See also *Ligia*, *Petrobius*, *Anurida*, *Orchestia* and *Littorina*.

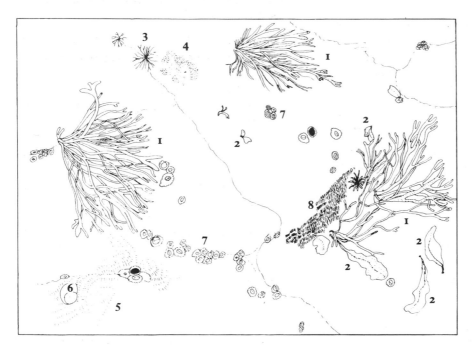

1 *Pelvetia canaliculata* (channel wrack)

2 young *Fucus spiralis* (spiral wrack)

3 young *Pelvetia*

4 *Verrucaria maura*

5 grazing marks (uneaten *Verrucaria*) left by periwinkles

6 *Littorina saxatilis* (rough periwinkle)

7 Acorn barnacles

8 *Lichina pygmaea*

PROBLEMS
- drying out (only 1–2 hours immersion due to the tides)
- short time to obtain nutrients from the water, thus slow growth and poor productivity
- wide variation in temperature possible affecting metabolism

---

Verrucaria maura
- ingrained black lichen, covering the bare rock
- terrestrial species capable of tolerating brief periods of salt-water cover
- edible to grazing animals after softening by water

Pelvetia canaliculata
(channel-wrack) up to 16 cm in length, bushy growth
- highest-level brown alga, indicating high water mark

Special adaptations
- the rolled fronds reduce water loss, trapping water face downwards
- a fatty (oily) layer over the cells slows desiccation
- a thick cell wall (1.2 μm) which shrinks with drying
- it survives a lower nutrient level than other large alga
- growth is slow but may continue at low tide
- rapid recovery of metabolism (e.g. photosynthesis) when tide returns, therefore a stress-tolerant alga, well adapted to a niche at the top of shore

Fucus spiralis
(spiral-wrack) up to 35 cm in length
- the spiraling frond not always present, the swollen tips are the reproductive structures
- it is a slightly lower level down the shore than *Pelvetia*, but with much overlap
- it has a thicker cell wall but lacks the oiliness of *Pelvetia*, so it loses water faster, hence the slightly lower shore level
- the spiraling traps water and slows evaporation but it is not as effective as *Pelvetia*
- growth is more rapid than *Pelvetia*; where overlap occurs, *Fucus* outshades the latter and then dominates
- shows better stress-tolerance than other wracks found further down shore

Lichina pygmaea
- a tufted, brown-black lichen, associated with barnacles
- it hides and supports a small animal community

Acorn barnacles
- the whiplash of algae may prevent larval settlement; attracted by the presence of adult barnacles
- white calcareous plates grow out and undercut the algal holdfast (competition)
- it is tolerant of high temperatures, e.g. *Chthamalus*: 50°C+
- it has a low metabolic rate i.e. slow heart rate and respiratory movement
- it can breathe atmospheric air at low tide, trapping bubbles with plates and releasing them with the return of the tide
- excretion continues at low tide; faecal pellets and shed exoskeleton are pushed out
- death leaves a cavity for colonisation, e.g. small periwinkles

Littorina saxatilis (Rough periwinkle)
- it grazes on algae and lichens (see radula marks)
- it has high temperature tolerance: at 36–38° C it crawls into crevices and becomes inactive
- in extremes of desiccation and temperature it cements itself to rock, respiring without oxygen, for up to a week
- the gills are modified to absorb air; they are capable of surviving one month out of water
- the adults mate and retain eggs to hatch inside the body; it has no need for sea-water for fertilisation or a planktonic life (lack of the latter reduces dispersal)
- it excretes insoluble uric acid to help conserve water

Radula marks
scrape marks left on the rocks after the radula (tongue) of a periwinkle has removed the fine growth of algae and lichens

SPECIES OF THE UPPER SHORE (*Pelvetia* and *F. spiralis* zone)

PLANTS

Lichens

Lichens are a symbiotic association between a fungus and an alga. The fungus possesses thick cell walls to reduce water loss and can store water (up to 3 times its own weight) as well as food produced by the algae.

Pelvetia canaliculata

The plants are hermaphrodite, having both male and female structures on the same frond. Conceptacles ripen in summer with the release of gametes in September to coincide with the high spring tides. Settlement of sporelings occur then but little development occurs until late winter. It takes twelve months to mature. Having both sexes on the same plant increases the chances of fertilisation on the upper shore where the tide does not give a long period of immersion. Light is an important factor in allowing good settlement of spores by stimulating growth of rhizoids which anchor the young plant to the rock.

F. spiralis

Like *Pelvetia* above, this plant is also hermaphrodite. No other species of *Fucus* is, however. The frond shows variation in its shape from one shore type to another and will be greatly affected by salinity and wave action. It also hybridises (crosses) with *F. vesiculosus* under certain conditions. Specimens at the bottom of the zone are less able to tolerate stress. This is due to individuals adapting (acclimatising) to the stresses over a period of weeks. This is not genetic and is similar to drought hardening.

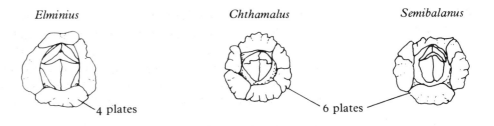

Elminius

Chthamalus

Semibalanus

4 plates

6 plates

ANIMALS

Acorn barnacles

Because they are cemented to the rock they form a distinct part of the zone. Internal fertilisation takes place from another barnacle less than 3.5 cm away. The eggs are retained inside the shell cavity until hatching into planktonic larvae (aids dispersal); they feed and go through six changes in the plankton before they settle on the shore, usually near to a group of existing adults. The adults feed on plankton when covered by seawater. The plates open to let the hairy legs draw in the filtered food. When the barnacles are left exposed, those individuals in regions of high humidity, e.g. in a small crevice, may develop a small hole to take in air to assist breathing. There is a correlation between the relative humidity of the atmosphere and the percentage of barnacles with the opening. Intense grazing by periwinkle and limpets may clear the rocks of algae and assist larval settlement.

Littorina (saxatilis) rudis

Natural selection in this most variable of zones has produced a 'complex' of variations in this species (many would say four separate species). Roughness of the shell increases with wave action, possibly for extra strength and also grip when washed into crevices. Those found amongst boulders and stones may lack the grooves on the shell completely. If dislodged and washed down the beach they are like all periwinkles and will migrate back; an important adaptation to maintain its position on the shore. This herbivore has many predators, especially sea-birds. It is a secondary host for a parasitic fluke whose eggs it consumes with its food. Gulls feeding on the periwinkle reinfect themselves and pass out of the eggs with their faeces which contaminate the food of the periwinkles.

ADDITIONAL SPECIES OF THE UPPER SHORE

PLANTS

Enteromorpha intestinalis

a long, green tubular alga, usually found in shallow pools
- it is very tolerant of environment changes e.g. salinity increase
- it grows where freshwater runs across the shore (good indicator)
- an early coloniser of bare rock, quick recolonisation after grazing
- it functions at low temperatures of $-21°C$, optimum: $17°C$
- it exhibits very rapid growth, a standing crop develops in 2 weeks
- it recovers quickly after exposure by the tide
- it starts life as two sheets of cells which fuse to form a tube, this inflates with oxygen as it photosynthesises, to keep it floating at the surface

Porphyra umbilicalis

a flat, sheet-like, red alga, usually found on the surface of rocks
- works best at low temperatures; most abundant in winter and spring
- it dries out at low tide but recovers very quickly afterwards
- an early coloniser of rock surfaces throughout shore
- it is mainly purple but can change the pigments in the cells (chromatic adaptation) to suit its position on the shore, it absorbs a wide range of wavelengths of the electromagnetic spectrum
- it is highly nutritious and is eaten by humans as laver

ANIMALS

Orchestia gammarella

commonly called sandhoppers, up to 20 mm in length
- usually found above the high tide mark under debris by day
- nocturnal feeders on alga freshly brought in by the tide
- it retreats to humid places by day to avoid desiccation therefore its behaviour is geared to day:night rhythms rather than tidal ones
- they flex their tails rapidly to escape predators, hence the common name

Ligia oceanica

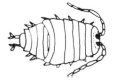

the common sea-slater, up to 25 mm in length
- it comes out mainly at night, thus avoiding predators and desiccation
- nocturnal scavengers on anything washed in by the tide, also carnivorous
- fast-moving animals without modified gills, needing periodic immersion
- unlike *Littorinids* in this region ammonia is excreted (not uric acid) which needs water; to adapt, they suppress their protein metabolism
- pale regions of the body are where shedding of the exoskeleton occurs

Anurida maritima

the marine springtail, one of the few insects of the seashore, 4 mm in length
- blue-black colouration, dense covering of hair, like velvet, enables it to live on the surface tension of small pools
- unlike most springtails, it cannot spring but crawls on the water surface; it is a scavenger, finding food by smell

Petrobius maritimus

the marine bristletail, a primitive marine insect, up to 10 mm in length
- a fast-moving, mainly nocturnal scavenger with large compound eyes
- it has biting mouthparts with long palps and sharp mandibles (closely resembling those of crustaceans)
- for rapid movement it needs warmth, absorbed from the sun-heated rock

Lasaea rubra

the commonest species on the seashore; a bivalve, 3 mm in length
- it lives in large numbers amongst the *Lichina* and empty barnacles
- usually found in clusters, attached by single byssus threads
- a suspension feeder, it can react very fast to the incoming tide so that no time is lost for feeding whilst covered
- negatively phototactic (moves away from light) keeping within its habitat
- it is a hermaphrodite with possible self-fertilisation (no planktonic larva)

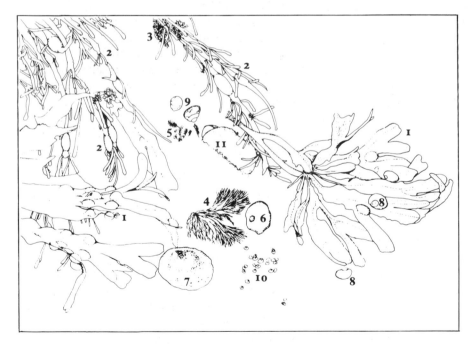

1 *Fucus vesiculosus* (bladder-wrack)

2 *Ascophyllum nodosum* (knotted wrack)

3 *Polysiphonia lanosa* (an epiphyte)

4 *Cladophora rupestris*

5 *Corallina officinalis*

6 *Actinia equina* (the beadlet anemone)

7 *Patella vulgata* (the common limpet) with black lichen on shell

8 *Littorina littoralis* (the flat periwinkle)

9 *Gibbula umbilicalis* (the purple topshell)

10 Acorn barnacle

11 *Cancer pagurus* (the edible crab)

- species are covered for half the day by the tide so desiccation problems are less severe than on the upper shore
- variable temperatures and humidity
- the light intensity reaching the algae is low at high tide

Ascophyllum nodosum

(knotted or egg-wrack) up to 2 m or more in length

- single, large air bladders float with fronds towards the light for maximum photosynthesis
- it can survive low temperatures, 10°C; breaking strain 37.6 kg cm^{-2}
- longevity: it lives for 15 years or more and thus competes favourably with other algae by forming a dominant blanket over the rocks
- little can grow below it and it may dominate sheltered shores
- it is easily cut by wave action due to the large surface area, note the broken tips
- it is unpalatable for most animals
- it is tolerant of shading
- the cell wall thickness is 1.02 μm

Fucus vesiculosus

(bladder-wrack) 20–75 cm in length

- it has pairs of air bladders which float with fronds towards the light
- many variants develop in response to salinity and wave action, e.g. bladderless form
- it grows rapidly after establishment, those on the edge of the distribution range may remain small
- breaking strain 45.5 kg cm^{-2}
- tolerant of freshwater, intolerant of desiccation
- cell wall thickness 0.69 μm
- replaces *Ascophyllum* lower down and in wave-exposed places

Gibbula umbilicalis (purple topshell) 1–2 cm

- a herbivore, feeding on the *Fucus*
- separate sexes release gametes into water for external fertilisation (planktonic larva)
- hollow spiral through the shell; a horny plate, the operculum, closes across the shell opening to reduce water loss at low tide

Cancer pagurus (edible crabs) and

Carcinus maenas (common shore crab)

- carnivores and scavengers
- *Cancer* has a pie-crust edge; *Carcinus* has 5 points on the carapace side near the eyes
- they are very mobile and can avoid some environmental stress by sheltering under large algae and stones, *Carcinus* is very adaptable and copes with varying salinity and temperature, see page 48

Littorina litoralis (flat periwinkle)

1 cm in length

- a herbivore, feeding on fucus, gaseous exchange via gills
- the periwinkle with least tolerance (of all periwinkles) of temperature and humidity variation
- the smooth, rounded shell blends with bladders of *Fucus*; numerous colour variations give camouflage at different seasons as algae varies, good example of polymorphism and natural selection
- the eggs are laid in gelatinous masses (prevents drying) on *Fucus* where they hatch into periwinkles (no larval form) directly onto food

Actinia equina

contracted (beadlet sea anemone)
2–7 cm in length

- copes with desiccation by contracting the tentacles inside, which reduces surface area; mucus reduces water loss further
- a carnivore feeding upon crustaceans, including crabs, shrimps and small fish
- gaseous exchange is by diffusion
- it is common under stones, ledges and seaweeds where humidity is high
- it attaches to the surface but can move

Cladophora rupestris

(dark green alga)

Patella vulgata

(common limpet) up to 4 cm in length

- it is a herbivore, feeding on microscopic algae attached to the rock surface, it may thus prevent the growth of larger seaweeds
- adhesion to the surface by the muscular foot and the secretion of a chemical
- hold on rock: 5.3 kg cm^{-2}
- clamping down at low tide prevents drying out, water is drawn into the gills via a hole above the head
- reduced metabolism when uncovered by tide

SPECIES OF THE MIDDLE SHORE
(*Ascophyllum* and *F. vesiculosus* zone)

PLANTS

Ascophyllum nodosum

The longest lived but least adaptable of the brown algae. It is a good indicator of sheltered shores where it will dominate. Sexes are separate and reproductive structures fall off after release of spores. This produces a weak thallus which allows entry of *Polysiphonia fastigiata* (a red alga) spores. Growth of this epiphyte may cause the death of the wrack in waves (heavy weight). Air bladders grow in a line along the frond, one per year. Colonisation beneath this wrack by other algae is difficult.

F. vesiculosus

Swollen conceptacles form at the tip of the frond and release spores in spring and summer, afterwards they decay and are lost. They live for about 3 years and grow 0.5 cm per week. They may become colonised by other algae, e.g. *Ectocarpus*. *F. vesiculosus* needs a high light intensity to grow well. The millions of spores released are rarely able to complete development; as they begin to grow they are consumed by limpets. These grazers will limit bladder-wrack considerably if their population density is high.

Cladophora rupestris

A common dark green alga of the middle and lower shore. It is a branched filamentous species giving a feathery appearance. Several dense layers of cellulose and a chitin-like material protect the alga from drying out. It is frequently found living under *Fucus* where it remains moist at low tide. A range of pigments absorb light in the shade of the *Fucus*.

ANIMALS

Crabs

Separate sexes mate, followed by the female carrying 800 000 eggs underneath the abdomen. A zoea larva hatches to live in the plankton as a carnivore. Survival is minimal and hence the large egg number. The edible crab is migratory, living and spawning offshore. When the larvae settle as young crabs on the seashore they feed and mature there, moving down into deeper water as they become adult. This avoids competition for food with young and adults on different sites. Crabs live for up to 4 years, ecdysing as necessary for growth. Soft 'peeler' crabs are those which have just undergone ecdysis. The shore crab is very variable in colour and is the most tolerant, of all crabs, to environmental stress.

Littorina littorea and L. obtusata

These are flat and edible periwinkles. Although both of these grazers live in the same region they do not compete. The former is the least tolerant of the periwinkles and relies on the humidity of the *Fucus* it is feeding upon for shelter. The latter is one of the most widespread species found on all seashores, even mud. It feeds by scraping the rock with its radula, often leaving marks. The heavy shell protects from drying and mechanical damage, with a cover – the operculum. Fertile eggs are released into the water and the larvae swim in amongst the plankton. It settles out on the shore and migrates up the beach, guided by responses to gravity and light. Both species have gills but can breathe for a period out of water.

Anemones

Exhibiting both asexual and sexual reproduction they rapidly colonise the shore. The beadlet is found the highest up the shore. It can survive out of water by withdrawing its tentacles. The snakeslock and others cannot do this and are usually restricted to rock pools and lower down. The sting cells (nematocysts) paralyse the prey and are triggered to fire by proteins on the food surface. They feel sticky to the touch as they fire the 'harpoons' into the skin. Beadlets are territorial, nudging each other (over a period of days) but snakeslocks form colonies of genetically identical individuals. Sperm are released by the male into the water. Here they swim and internally fertilise the female. She eventually releases minute sea anemones. Asexual budding also occurs.

Patella vulgata	The limpet is not restricted to any one zone, it is able to cope with most of the limiting factors of the seashore. The muscular foot creates a 'vacuum' and by clamping down at low tide drying out is prevented; limpets rotate the shell and grind it into the rock producing a good fit. On death it leaves a scar. It grazes on the surface of the rock scraping away any microscopic algae, leaving marks. It is the most important herbivore in restricting the growth of algae; comparable to the rabbit restricting growth of grass in meadows. Often the only algae to be found is that growing on the shell where they cannot reach. The shell shape varies with wave action, it is flat in sheltered conditions and domed in wave action. This is the indirect effect of muscles pulling down during wave action, producing the dome shape. Sexes are separate but as in many molluscs they often begin life as males changing to a female. The larvae live in the plankton for barely two weeks.

ADDITIONAL SPECIES OF THE MIDDLE SHORE

PLANTS

Ulva lactuca

the sea lettuce, up to 40 cm in length, it is a light green alga
- it recovers quickly from desiccation to full metabolism
- the frond is a sheet of undifferentiated tissue, 2 cells thick
- very abundant under brown algae, and if nitrate level high

Ceramium rubrum

1–30 cm in length, a red alga, often growing attached to other algae
- branched, filamentous with curled-in tips. See also *Laurencia, Lomentaria, Chondrus, Corallina, Nemalion* and *Lithophyllum*.

ANIMALS

Mytilus edulis

the common or blue mussel, 1–10 cm in length
- it attaches itself to the rock by threads secreted by the byssus gland which is located on the foot; breaking and producing new byssus threads allows minor movement
- two shells give protection and close at low water to retain water, under stress metabolism drops to conserve energy
- the larvae settle out of water, triggered by a negative response to light, roughness of the substrate increases settlement
- they are filter feeders, water is drawn in through siphons, those living higher up the shore are smaller as feeding time is less; the foot can be extended out of the shell, wiped over its outer surface where detritus settles, and drawn in
- eaten by dog-whelks, starfish, oyster-catchers and eider ducks

Thais (Nucella) lapillus

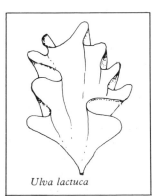

Ulva lactuca

the dog-whelk, 1–3 cm in length, distinct groove across shell lip
- a carnivore, it eats barnacles, limpets and mussels; the radula is modified for shell boring, chemical means assist; the shell (siphon) groove allows water in for gaseous exchange
- very adaptable feeders, changing diet according to availability
- eggs are laid in capsules of 100s, most are infertile; only a few mini-adults emerge, they feed on the infertile eggs
- the young migrate to the lower shore to feed, moving up as they mature
- found on all rocky shores with a wide variation in shell size, shape and thickness; a thicker shell gives protection from crabs on sheltered shores (see page 19)

See also acorn barnacles, blenny and oystercatcher.

LOWER SHORE COMMUNITY

N.B. *F. serratus* has been moved to show the community beneath

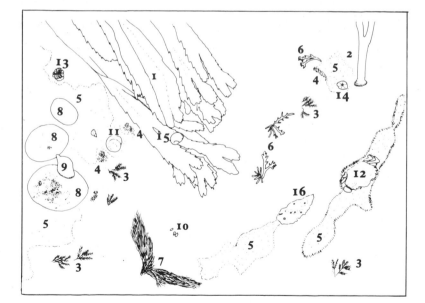

1 *Fucus serratus* (saw wrack)

2 holdfast and stipe of *F. serratus*

3 *Corallina officinalis* (dominant ground cover under *F. serratus*)

4 stunted *Corallina*

5 *Lithophyllum* sp., the expanse to the left has been bleached by sunlight

6 *Laurencia pinnatifida* (pepper dulse)

7 *Cladophora rupestris*

8 *Patella vulgata* (common limpet) with black lichen on shell

9 *Thais lapillus* (dog-whelk) eating limpet

10 Egg capsules of the dog-whelk

11 *Gibbula umbilicalis* (purple topshell)

12 *Carcinus maenas* (common shore crab)

13 *Anemonia viridis* (the snakeslock anemone) collapsed

14 *Bunodactis verrucosa* (gem anemone) collapsed

15 *Littorina littoralis* (flat periwinkle)

16 *Halichondria panicea* (bread crumb sponge)

- relatively stable environment with a high productivity, this means that more organisms compete for space, food, etc.
- light intensity diminishes at high tide because of the depth of water, photosynthesis can only occur when covered by water
- cloudy (turbid) water will reduce the light levels further and restrict the numbers of species able to survive here

Fucus serratus

(the saw or toothed-wrack) 50–80 cm in length

- the commonest species of the lower shore and partly uncovered at neap tides; it lives for 3 years, on slow-draining shores it may occupy a third of the area of the seashore
- intolerant of desiccation, the cell wall is only 0.42 μm thick
- the fronds are flat and at low tide only the top surface frond dries
- growth, shape of frond and breeding pattern is variable, this is related to climate and temperature, e.g. fronds are longer with less branches in Scotland compared with shorter, branched individuals in Devon, England
- after the tide returns recovery to full metabolism is the slowest of the fucoid algae
- it is intolerant of heavy wave action, and is replaced by Himanthalia elongata under these conditions
- like many algae of the lower shore it adapts to low light intensity by developing additional pigments for absorbing maximum light
- fronds are often colonised by Spirorbis, small polychaete worms which secrete a calcareous, spiralled tube (diameter 3 mm) and are filter feeders
- the flat fronds also prevent the area around the alga from drying out, numerous organisms will colonise this space

Corallina officinalis

a calcareous red alga, 4–10 cm in length

- a chalky alga which covers a wide area of the shore but survives best lower down where it shows up darker red; it bleaches in the sun
- it forms a dense turf under the dominant brown algae, thus it grows better in exposed areas where fewer browns will shade them
- intolerant of desiccation (it turns white)
- tolerates wave action and shade

Patella vulgata

(common limpet)

- grazes on microscopic algae, black lichen grows on its shell
see page 17

Laurencia pinnatifida

(pepper dulse) 2–10 cm in length

- flattened, branched frond of variable colour depending on exposure to light, it becomes bleached to yellow-white
- it forms dense turf under brown algae; it is shade tolerant

Lithophyllum species

a calcareous red alga encrusting on the rock

- rock-like pink alga, white at the edge where bleached and dried
- resistant to grazing and tolerant of shade and wave action
- Lithothamnion is a similar species
- in the water-covered crevices, under the Fucus, both calcareous algae are the best adapted species to survive the very low light level; their colour is dark red compared to the bleached white of the specimen to the left of the photograph

Halichondria panicea

(bread-crumb sponge)

- lies within crevices to avoid desiccation
- the holes on the surface (oscula) pass water and waste out; fresh seawater is absorbed through the surface
- Grantia compressa is a second common species of sponge, present here attached to the base of the Corallina; flattened with a single osculum at the apex

Anemonia viridis

(the snakeslock anemone)

- unlike the beadlet anemone higher up the shore, it is unable to contract the tentacles reduce surface area and water loss
- it prevents significant water loss by living in crevices or under the Fucus

Bunodactis verrucosa

(the gem anemone)

- small anemone which is well camouflaged living amongst Corallina and Lithophyllum
- like the beadlet anemone it is ovoviviparous, i.e. fertile eggs are retained by female until they are miniature adults, this increases chances of embryo survival and the recolonisation of the seashore

SPECIES OF THE LOWER SHORE (*F. serratus* zone)

PLANTS

F. serratus

A thick midrib is in the centre of a frond edged with serrations. However, it is softer than the other fucoids. The sexes are separate, unlike the fucoids of the upper shore, and the concepta are more streamlined at the tips. Like the bladder-wrack, female gametes produce chemical attractants (pheromones) called fucoserratin, to attract the males.

The red algae

This zone sees the start of those species producing a turf underneath the dominant brown algae. They are all typically shade tolerant and with an accessory pigment, **phycoerythrin**, are able to photosynthesise under very low light levels. They are all prone to bleaching in high illumination. *Corallina* and *Lithothamnion* have a high chalk content as a by-product of metabolism and are very tough, making them resistant to wave action as well as to grazing in this rich community.

Light and the algae

Absorption of light on the lower shore depends on whether additional pigments are available for photosynthesis. Blue light, the part of the spectrum used by most land plants, is reflected away at the water surface and the mid band of the visible spectrum is largely unabsorbed. Three additional or **accessory pigments** are synthesised by the algae in the lower shore: fucoxanthin, phycoerythrin and phycocyanin. These absorb predominantly green light. It it noticeable how the algae appear much darker in the lower shore due to the considerable absorption of light. Plants moved lower down the shore increase the production of the accessory pigment.

ADDITIONAL SPECIES OF THE LOWER SHORE

PLANTS

Himanthalia (elongata) lorea

(thongweed) up to 1 m in length, it is a brown alga

● in the first year of growth it is just a small button, like a mushroom, 2 cm across, in the second year a branching frond grows from the centre, conceptacles are based on this

● its presence is characteristic of extreme wave action, where it replaces the toothed-wrack in dominating this part of the shore; the two species compete for the same niche but thongweed has a wider stress tolerance. However, it is not normally seen with the wrack

Comparison of the two seaweeds in varying wave action:

extreme wave action ⟵   ⟶ extreme shelter

Himanthalia: ■■ ■■ ■■■■■■■■ ■■■   ■   ■ ■ ■ ■■■■■
F. serratus: ■ ■■■■■■■■■■■■■■■■■ ■■ ■ ■■

Theoretically thongweed should be found on all shores with its wide tolerance. *F. serratus* grows quickly; if the buttons of thongweed are beneath they will be shaded out and killed. Therefore, where they compete the wrack will win; only when the conditions become extreme can the thongweed survive as the wrack disappears.

Codium tomentosum

branched, spongy green alga, up to 30 cm in length

● grows singly beneath the brown algae, high concentration of chlorophyll a, it has a dark appearance as it is able to absorb much light with an action potential similar to *Laminaria*

See also *Chondrus, Gigartina, Cladophora, Ulva* and *Ceramium*.

ANIMALS

Encrusting sponges

The bread-crumb sponge is common under the humid fronds of the wrack, filling the crevices with its yellow or green asymmetrical mass. It is also found in deep clefts and overhangs of rock where water continues to drip. When covered by the tide it filters the water for plankton and detritus. It is very sensitive to desiccation. Oxygen is obtained by diffusion. Although hermaphrodite, the gonads ripen at different times ensuring cross-fertilisation.

Hydroids

Polyps:
Dynamena (right)
and *Obelia* (left)

Several species of hydroid grow attached to the seaweeds or rock. The colony consists of a stalk from which project asexual polyps, these feeding stages produce sexual stages called medusae. This dispersal stage produces gametes and after fertilisation a larva hatches settling on the shore. Guided by positive phototaxis it moves about and eventually attaches itself permanently and develops a new colony. Feeding is like the sea anemones and food is passed along the colony.

Bryozoans or sea-mat
e.g. *Membranipora*

These minute organisms form flat colonies over the survace of seaweeds. The animals live in chambers of calcium carbonate and filter the seawater for food. They are hermaphrodite and fertilisation occurs within the colony before release. Asexual reproduction increases the area of colony across the substrate.

Pomatoceros triqueter

a calcareous tube worm; 3–6 cms in length, the tube is triangular in section

- a crown of tentacles filter water for food and absorb oxygen

Scale worms

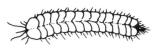

Polychaetes with dorsal scales, the number and size varies with the species

- they live under stones and seaweeds searching for prey
- after mating the female retains the eggs which thus avoid entering the plankton; the larvae are shed directly onto the substrate

Archidoris pseudoargus

(sea-lemon) a sea-slug, up to 7 cm in length

- the shell is absent, 9 gills are arranged in a circle around the anus; they are usually found on the shore in summer when they spawn
- they feed on sponges, the surface is warty with internal chalky deposits

Aeolidia papillosa

(grey sea-slug) up to 10 cm in length, common under stones

- it feeds on sea anemones whose sting cells are undigested and transported intact to the dorsal surface to be used for defence
- spawning occurs in summer, spawn contain 400 000 eggs

Blennius pholis
(See photo page 38)

(common blenny or shanny) 5–10 cms in length, commonest littoral fish

- it is able to survive out of water at low tide
- powerful jaws for crushing barnacles (main diet), crabs, algae
- after hatching the young feed offshore and move back to the shore when mature

Oystercatcher

a black and white bird with long red bill; 40 cm in length

- carnivore of the lower shore, it feeds on shellfish, especially mussels; the powerful, sensitive bill regrows to allow for wear
- the bill shape varies according to diet, soft food results in a slim bill, hard foods produce a 'hammer' bill
- it nests on the shore when 3 years old; the young are fed by adults for up to a year

LAMINARIA ZONE — the transition of littoral to sublittoral

Laminaria zone: general view at low, spring tide

PROBLEMS and FEATURES of the zone

- relatively constant environment
- it is rarely uncovered except by an extreme low tide
- wave action is at its greatest and most intense
- greatest depth of water, light is at a minimum
- highest productivity (photosynthesis) of any zone partly due to the long immersion time enabling organisms to obtain nutrients for growth
- the competition is intense as the conditions are least stressful

Laminaria
hyperborea

Laminaria
digitata

Laminaria
saccharina

The three Laminarian species compared

The dominant brown algae in the *Laminaria* zone

The lamina or blade
- for photosynthesis, it is supported by the water
- it is shed from the stipe each autumn to reduce surface area, the plant therefore dislodges in winter gales
- if not shed, a second lamina grows beneath the first to form a double blade

The stipe
- gives support
- the tip regrows a lamina each spring

The holdfast
- gives firm attachment to the substrate

GENERAL FEATURES OF THE LAMINARIANS OR KELP

- kelp beds are like a marine forest with layers of algae and animals
- they cannot tolerate any degree of desiccation
- growth is prolific: most of the productivity is from the continuously growing lamina which grows at the base and erodes at the tip like a conveyor belt
- structurally the most advanced of the algae, the trumpet shaped cells in the stipe are believed to have a conducting function
- they exhibit alternation of generations, the dominant phase (the kelp plant) is the sporophyte, this bears sporangia which release zoospores into the water, these germinate to produce a gameteophyte stage, of which little is known
- sporangia develop on both sides of the lamina surface
- a cross-section through the stipe reveals annual growth rings, the average age is about five years
- kelps are harvested commercially for alginates (used in cosmetics, toothpaste and ice cream), potash, soda, iodine and animal fodder
- all adapt well to low light intensities
- in very sheltered conditions the lower shore may be sand or mud, the deposition of material will replace the kelps by *Zostera* (eel grass); if small stones are present, *Chorda filum* (bootlace weed) grows

Laminaria saccharina

(sugar kelp or sea-belt) up to 2 m in length

- unlike the other kelps the lamina is a continuous ribbon with a frilled edge, the central part is thickened
- the holdfast is branched but very small in comparison with the other kelps
- unable to cope with intense wave action it is limited to sheltered regions and deep rock pools
- it is called the sugar kelp because when it is dry a white, sugary substance develops on the surface
- the stipe is flexible so at low tide the plant goes limp and lies flat, thus remaining in the shallow water

Laminaria digitata

(tangle or oarweed) about 1 m in length

- the lamina is split into many 'digits', splitting increases with the wave action
- the holdfast is very branched and broad giving stronger attachment to the rock than *L. saccharina*
- the stipe is flexible so at low tide the plant goes limp and lies flat, thus remaining in the shallow water and not drying out
- the stipe is smooth and oval in section, its length varies with depth of water
- these listed features enable it to survive a high degree of wave action, on very sheltered shores it may grow as a single blade

Laminaria hyperborea

(the cuvie) 1–3 m in length

- the lamina is split which reduces the effects of wave action
- the holdfast is huge and dome-shaped giving the best attachment in extremes of wave action
- the stipe is inflexible supporting the kelp upright, this would cause the alga to dry out, it survives, therefore, only in the sublittoral zone where it will be unaffected by the tides; the spray from extreme wave action may push a small number onto the lower shore
- the stipe surface is rough enabling red algae to colonise it, *Rhodymenia pseudopalmata* is a common epiphyte here; the stipe is round in section
- typically found in deep water offshore and in areas of turbulent or heavy wave action

SPECIES OF THE LAMINARIA ZONE

PLANTS

Laminaria species

Their name is given to the zone as they dominate this region of the sublittoral edge. *L. digitata* and *L. saccharina* live at the low water spring tides mark or higher if in a deep rock pool. The latter species is restricted to sheltered places but the former is widespread; in deep water it is restricted by competition with *L. hyperborea*. This species grows long, rigid stipes in deep water and soon shades out the other kelps. Kelps growing in deeper water develop more pigment than those higher up to enable them to absorb what little light there is. Many organisms colonise the kelp both for space and food, e.g. sea mat grows on the lamina to gain access to circulating water containing their food. The blue-rayed limpet feeds on the kelp. The holdfast is a **microhabitat** containing a micro-community. Based on plankton as the producer, the primary consumers are thousands of sedentary polychaete worms which filter the water. Most of these worms are minute. Small brittlestars also filter feed. Large carnivorous polychaetes feed on the sedentary worms; at the top of this food web is the hairy crab (*Pilumnis hirtellus*), one or two may live under each holdfast.

ADDITIONAL SPECIES OF THE LAMINARIA ZONE

PLANTS

The red algae

As depth increases the red algae become more dominant. *Chondrus crispus* and *Gigartina stellata* form dense tufts around the base of the kelp. *Rhodymenia pseudopalmata* often grows attached to the kelp as a way of reaching the light. All have accessory pigments (page 22) contained in cell organelles called phycobilisomes. These pigments absorb light and pass the energy via a chain reaction to the chlorophyll a for photosynthesis. The red algae are very shade tolerant living under the kelp, and require a fraction of the light used by land plants. In fact, if the light is too intense it soon becomes bleached, the tips of *Chondrus* are often white or yellow. *Chondrus* may dominate the smaller algae as few herbivores will graze upon it.

Chondrus crispus   Gigartina stellata   Rhodymenia pseudopalmata

Saccorhiza bulbosa

(the furbelows) largest European seaweed, up to 5 m in length

- an annual plant, very fast growing
- the flat stipe is rigid with ruffles which dissipate wave energy so it can survive the surf, the holdfast is bulbous – nearly a metre in diameter when fully grown
- the rigid stipe does not enable it to avoid desiccation
- the short-lived holdfast is not colonised by a micro-community
- it usually forms a community with *L. hyperborea* in deep water but often extends onto the lower shore if spray allows

See also *Lithophyllum, Codium, Cladophora, Ulva* and *Corallina*.

ANIMALS

A wide diversity of animals live in this zone because of the abundance of food and because it is the least stressful region in which to live. Few show adaptations to survive varying abiota. It is the competition for food and space which dominates life. Only a limited variety of animals are discussed here.

Paddle worms

Predatory polychaetes with flattened parapodia used in swimming
Eulalia viridis (green leaf worm) up to 14 cm in length

- a long and very thin, bright green worm actively crawling over rocks and holdfasts in search of sponges, its main prey

Topshells

Important herbivores, two species are particularly common
Gibbula cineraria (grey topshell) 1.25 cm in length

- it lacks the purple banding of *G. umbilicalis* and the hole beneath the shell is small, lacks the stress tolerance shown in other topshell species

Calliostoma zizyphinum (painted topshell) 2 cm in length

- a beautiful cone-shaped shell, common amongst holdfasts
- unlike other topshells the larval stage is absent, mini-adults are born directly onto the shore

Patina pellucida

(blue-rayed limpet) 0.5–1.5 cm in length

- small, transparent individuals, common on the blades of kelp where they rasp away forming depressions, feeding as they go – this may weaken the frond or stipe; with the shedding of kelp blades in autumn the limpet is lost
- a subspecies, *P. pellucida laevis*, in response to changing day length, exhibits positive geotaxis usually ending up in the holdfast where it resumes feeding, weakening the holdfast

Sea-urchins

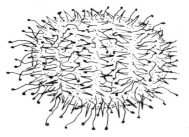

The echinoderm species in general are found in this region; none can survive long out of water. The tube feet enable the urchin to anchor itself to the substrate in the surf.
Echinus esculentus (edible sea-urchin) 6–12 cm in diameter

- because of its large size it represents the most important grazer since it can cause considerable damage to the kelp forest
- adversely affected by high temperatures and in southern regions of the British Isles it is restricted to deep water

Psammechinus miliaris (green sea-urchin) 4 cm in diameter

- found higher on the shore, particularly around *Corallina*, where it feeds on both plant and animals, these includes barnacles mussels, sponges and hydroids

Asterias rubens

(common starfish) 5–30 cm in diameter

- the tube feet are used in feeding as well as for attachment to the rock, it feeds by inverting the stomach onto the food which consists of soft-bodied animals, e.g. sponges, sea-squirts, hydroids; mussel shells are opened by the tube feet on the 'arms'
- digestion is outside the body
- there are separate sexes and fertilisation is external producing planktonic larvae

Brittle stars

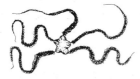

- it resembles starfish but breaks its arms off if handled roughly (autotomy)
- it filters water for plankton and detritus, larger ones feed on dead animals

See also sea anemones, *Archidoris*, bryozoa, *Mytilus*, crabs and scale worms.

ZONATION ON THE ROCKY SHORE

General features to look for:

- productivity is low on the upper shore, it increases towards the lower shore
- descending the shore there is an increase in species and community complexity
- competition increases towards the lower shore
- there is a marked banding of the communities on the seashore

There is no one reason for the zonation that is so well marked on rocky shores. It is the result of interactions between a number of physical, chemical and biotic factors. We must consider

1 the limiting factors in this ecosystem
2 the adaptations of the organisms to the factors.

Zonation of brown algae from upper shore (left) to lower shore (right)

Pelvetia *F. spiralis* *F. vesiculosus* *Ascophyllum* *F. serratus* *Laminaria*

	Pelvetia	Fucus spiralis	Ascophyllum	Fucus vesiculosus	Fucus serratus	Laminaria
cell wall thickness / μm	1.2	1.47	1.02	0.69	0.42	–
% metabolism recovery after reimmersion	95%	49%	35%	20%	0	0
wavelength of light required for full photosynthesis	–	–	–	600	500	150
reproduction: hermaphrodite or sexes	herm	herm	sep	sep	sep	sep

Zonation of periwinkles and topshells from upper shore (left) to lower shore (right)

L. rudis *L. littorea* *L. obtusata* *G. umbilicalis* *Calliostoma*

	L. neritoides	L. rudis	L. littorea G. umbilicalus	L. obtusata	Calliostoma
nitrogenous excretory product	uric acid	uric acid	ammonia	ammonia	ammonia
main diet	lichens	lichens /micro algae	micro /macro algae	*Fucus*	red /green algae
lethal limit of temperature /°C	46.3	45	L = 46 G = 42	44	34.5
water loss per day as % of body weight	3.7%	5.6%	5.35%	8.35%	–

SUMMARY OF LIMITING FACTORS AFFECTING ZONATION

1 **Desiccation**, as a result of exposure at low tide, influences the upper and middle shore zonation

2 **Wave action** increases humidity (see separate section, page 31).

3 **Light** is needed for photosynthesis. All seaweeds need to be in water for this to occur. The water will filter off some of the wavelengths of light and reduce the intensity. Smaller algae, for example the red algae, will photosynthesise with 10% of the light required by the brown algae. The **compensation point** for *Laminaria* is only 320 lux, a typical land plant is nearer 1800 lux.

4 **Temperature** Immersion in water buffers against temperature change and so upper shore species will have to tolerate the greatest variation. It will also affect the rate of metabolism. Bladder-wrack can just respire at 17°C, *Enteromorpha* at −22°C, 17°C is optimum. High temperatures will increase drying out and increase salinity in pools due to evaporation of water.

5 **Aspect** is the direction in which the shore faces. A southern aspect has more illumination and warmth, but dries faster; a northern aspect is cooler and darker. Thus on a north facing slope community bands will be wider and higher up.

6 **Slope** A flatter shore will expose a greater area of substrate for colonising and will not drain as fast as a steeper one.

7 **Turbidity** is the cloudiness of the water. Large amounts of plankton can increase the turbidity, as will detritus and sewage pollution. This restricts the intensity of light reaching the algae on the rocks.

8 **Substrate** The hardness and particle size of rock will influence the ability of an organism to attach itself. Soft rocks will be suitable for burrowers, e.g. piddocks. Large boulders and rocks give greater shelter for animals and the angle of the rock strata may produce more crevices and pools.

9 **Freshwater** Seepage of water from the cliff can dilute the seawater. Few of the organisms on the shore can tolerate salinity changes. *Enteromorpha* is so tolerant it is a good indicator of freshwater on rocky shores. Upper shore rockpools are particularly vulnerable to salinity variation.

10 **Biotic** These are the biological factors influencing the community. Grazing is perhaps the most important to consider, herbivores will often determine the presence or absence of the dominant seaweeds. (Feeding and competition is dealt with further on.) Algal turf, e.g. *Laurencia* and *Chondrus*, will slow down the drainage on the shore and reduce desiccation. The fucoids have a 'whiplash' effect: water movement causes a sweeping action of the algae across the substrate and prevents the attachment of spores and larvae.

ORGANISM ADAPTATION AND COMPETITION FOR RESOURCES

Organisms are rarely able to live in a variety of environmental conditions, having adapted to a narrow range by natural selection. As a result each occupies a specific niche. Spores and larvae may be deposited on any part of the seashore but they will only develop if the conditions there allow them to. Laminarian spores do settle on the upper shore whilst *Pelvetia* spores do settle on the lower. It would be unlikely if they grew because *Laminaria* cannot survive drying and *Pelvetia* could not cope with the competition; where one performs well another will find it lethal. In this way organisms become partitioned into zones where they do best. There will be some overlap and where this occurs each organism is at the edge of its niche, that is at the limit of the conditions which it can tolerate. Consequently they may not be typical specimens but poorly developed variations, e.g. mussels on the upper shore are small as they do not obtain enough food.

SEDENTARY ORGANISMS

tend to be more highly specialised than mobile ones. Barnacles are the only species that can maintain life at 50°C. Mobile animals can move away from stressful situations; fish move with the tide and crabs will shelter under rocks. Zonation in animals is best seen in the static species which, like the algae, are anchored to the rock and must tolerate the micro-climate. Animals that do move have the potential problem of straying from their niche.

MAINTENANCE OF ZONATION

is crucial. Animal movements are controlled by taxes (responses to light, gravity and humidity) which change, often with the state of the tide. This helps to keep the organism in the conditions which suit it best. Edible periwinkles constantly stray from their niche.

Resources in an ecosystem, e.g. space, light

and food, are limited. Organisms compete for these resources. Specialisations like faster growth rate, will help the competitor to win and dominate over its rival in a constant environment. (See thongweed and tooth wrack page 22.)

INTERSPECIFIC COMPETITION

This is the competition between different species. Better feeding efficiency and reproductive rate will help the winner. But if conditions were to vary such specialisations become a hindrance. *F. spiralis* will shade *Pelvetia* on the upper shore, *Ascophyllum* shades out *F. vesiculosus* in the middle and Laminarians with a flexible stipe survive over the rigid variety. The fucoids with the whiplash prevent barnacles from settling and as barnacles grow their plates 'move' across the rock cutting off any attached algae. The two species of barnacle, *Chthamalus* and *Semibalanus*, compete for space in the upper and middle shores. The former is more tolerant of drying as it has a non-porous shell, an operculum, high temperature tolerance and the larvae settle out of the plankton on just a film of water. Hence, it is

found on the highest part of the beach. As it merges with the *Semibalanus* population it begins to lose the battle because all those specialisations are at the expense of growing slowly. The shell of *Semibalanus* is porous but quick to grow and soon cuts out the competitor. *Semibalanus* is restricted by dog-whelk predation. Competition in overlapping niches has thus led to zonation of the barnacles.

INTRASPECIFIC COMPETITION

Competition is greatest with members of the same species. Older plants will shade out younger ones which try to develop below their fronds. Only after the death of the plant will spores have a chance to grow.

Animals usually have the ability to move away from a competitor and in this instance we see territorial behaviour. Beadlet sea anemones have been shown to butt each other over a period of time with the weaker individual moving away. Anemones on an overhang of rock may have a regular distribution pattern – all a similar distance apart.

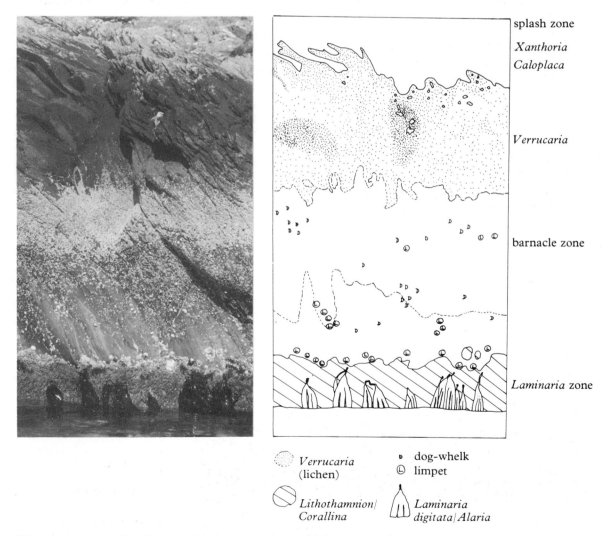

splash zone
Xanthoria
Caloplaca

Verrucaria

barnacle zone

Laminaria zone

Verrucaria (lichen)

dog-whelk

limpet

Lithothamnion/ Corallina

Laminaria digitata/Alaria

Zonation on a rocky shore which is exposed to a high degree of wave action

FEATURES OF THE WAVE-EXPOSED ROCKY SHORE

- *Verrucaria* and *Littorina* zone extensive
- note the poor growth of seaweed and therefore low productivity
- there is an absence of fucoid algae, these are replaced by a barnacle zone
- the lower limit of the barnacles will be determined by the dog-whelks
- mussels and occasionally beadlet sea anemones are found in crevices
- the limpets are *Patella aspera* which have a thicker shell than *P. vulgata* and are able to withstand a greater force
- note the attached *Laminaria* with their large holdfasts and the encroaching *Alaria esculenta* which has a very strong midrib
- *Corallina* and *Lithothamnion* form the dominant algae of the shore
- on a more gradual slope *Himanthalia* would form a zone near the red algal zone

THE EFFECT OF WAVE ACTION ON ZONATION

The communities described so far are the most typical. Increased or decreased action of waves will have a modifying effect on the communities changing the species such that it may be un-recognisable (see facing page).

Examples of modifications include:

1 A change in the dominant community by removal of competitor species.

- large surface areas are a disadvantage with wave action: *F. serratus* will be removed, favouring *Himanthalia*; *Ascophyllum* tolerates little action and *F. vesiculosus* takes over; *Laminaria* is replaced by *Alaria* in extremes
- *Patella vulgata* is replaced by *P. aspera* which is able to exert a greater suction to the rock for attachment; barnacles and mussels increase

2 The shape and form of growth e.g. bladder-wrack and limpets

- bladder-wrack varies in the number of airbladders; production reduces with wave action to in extreme cases it becomes a bladder-less variety.
- limpet shells are flat in shelter, domed with wave action (see page 19)

3 Productivity decreases with increased wave action

- most of the larger seaweeds cannot remain attached as wave action increases
- mainly calcareous, small, slow-growing seaweeds survive

4 Displacement of zonation up the shore and extension of the splash zone

- waves will increase the humidity on the shore so that desiccation is less of a problem: algae and animals survive further up the beach; *Laminaria* may remain uncovered at low tide as the spray keeps them wet
- the spray up the cliff will extend the *Verrucaria* and *Littorina* zone

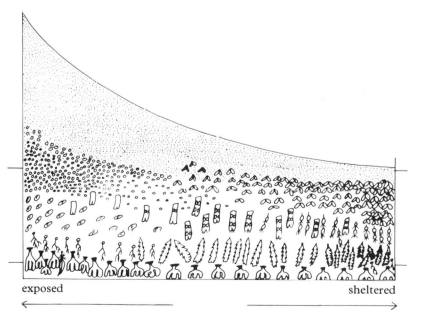

	Verrucaria
∞	*F. spiralis*
○	barnacle
	Ascophyllum nodosum
	F. vesiculosus
	F. vesiculosus var. *linearis*
	F. serratus
	Himanthalia elongata
	Laminaria
∂	*Mytilus edulis*
	Alaria esculenta

exposed   sheltered

Fig. 6 A simplified diagrammatic interpretation of wave action on zonation

FEEDING RELATIONSHIPS ON THE ROCKY SHORE

The algae absorb sunlight by photosynthesis and convert solar energy into chemical energy which they use or store within the cell. They are the primary producers within this ecosystem. However, the algae exist in many forms. Seaweeds produce thousands of cells on the frond surface which, like human skin cells, erode away from the plant. The tips of *Laminaria* blades erode continually; 40% of the productivity of *Ascophyllum* is lost to the sea. These cells become suspended in the water and subject to bacterial action. They are filtered and consumed by animals. The surface of the rock may appear to be devoid of algae but will have a fine layer of microscopic blue-green algae.

The food sources available to herbivorous animals in this ecosystem are

- macroscopic algae or seaweeds e.g. *Fucus, Laminaria*
- microscopic algae e.g. *Calothrix* and blue-green algae
- diatoms in the phytoplankton
- cells in suspension and cells converted to detritus by bacteria
- lichens e.g. *Verrucaria*

The sea is one of the most productive of ecosystems; phytoplankton reproduce very quickly; *Saccorhiza* grows to over five metres in length in a year and weighs several kilograms.

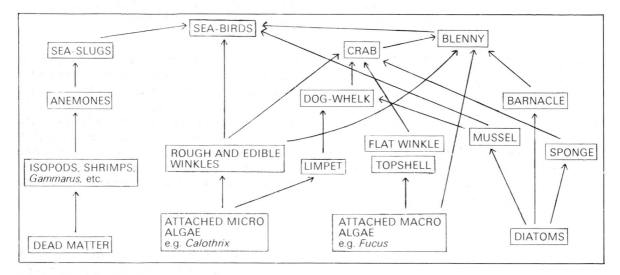

Fig. 7   Simplified food web on a rocky shore

FACTORS AFFECTING THE FOOD WEB

- algae, with some exceptions, grow best in summer; some animals only appear on the seashore when spawning occurs e.g. sea-slugs; land birds often come on to the shore to feed in winter when the fields are covered by snow
- animal density varies and a predator will usually take those prey which are easiest to come by i.e. the most abundant, this may mean an alternative to the usual diet
- crude oil adheres to the rock and by covering any lichens will prevent photosynthesis; trampling by humans will prevent spores developing and reduce productivity of the shore: reduction in top carnivores (sea-birds) by oil pollution will give an expansion in the number of prey items below them in the web
- foreign species will not fit into any particular zone and may take over dominance, killing species off indiscriminately e.g. *Sargassum muticum* or Jap Weed, arrived on the south coast in 1970, seashores around the Isle of Wight and other localities became swamped, as the weed shaded out natural communities

FEEDING MECHANISMS USED BY ANIMALS ON THE ROCKY SHORE

1 Plankton and detritus feeders
   - gills e.g. mussels
   - appendages e.g. barnacles use limbs
   - pores e.g. sponges
   - tentacles e.g. sedentary polychaete worms
   - perforated pharynx e.g. sea-squirts
   - cilia e.g. brittle stars
2 Debris feeders (scavengers)
   - mouthparts and pincers e.g. crabs
3 Seaweed feeders
   - grazing gastropod molluscs using a radula e.g. topshells and periwinkles
4 Predators
   - shell borers e.g. dog-whelk, with radula and chemicals
   - shell openers e.g. starfish, tube feet and inverted gut
   - paralysis of prey e.g. sea-anemones, with nematocysts
   - capture of prey e.g. cuttlefish, with tentacles e.g. blenny, with teeth on powerful jaw e.g. cormorant and gulls with beak

PREDATION AND ITS EFFECT ON DIVERSITY

The richness of the species within a habitat will depend on (a) food preferences and (b) the intensity of grazing.

Fig. 8 demonstrates the effect that increasing predation has upon the richness of species in a community such as that found on the lower shore. In this region several seaweeds are in competition. With a minimum of grazing a wide choice of food is available and a preference for particular algae results in the least favoured one becoming dominant (e.g. *Chondrus crispus*). As grazing increases so all the algae will be affected and will be present. If overgrazing occurs then algae may never reach maturity, spores are eaten before they can grow and only a few, grazing-tolerant species survive. Compare these facts with Fig. 9.

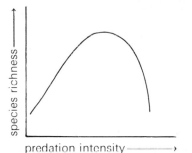

Fig. 8 The effect of predation on richness of species

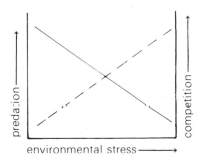

Fig. 9 Predation and competition in relationship to the degree of environmental stress

PARASITISM

Feeding relationships are inevitably one-sided; the dog-whelk kills the barnacle and consumes it in one go, then moving on to another one. It therefore lives on 'capital'. Parasitism is a nutritional method whereby the organism does not kill the prey but lives upon it, thereby living on a 'steady income'. Parasites are very specialised for this existence and invariably modify the host. The crab, *Carcinus*, is affected by a barnacle-type parasite, *Sacculina*. The name is derived from a yellow sac attached to the underside of the crab's abdomen. It looks nothing like a barnacle. Feeding on the crab causes many physiological and behavioural changes e.g. stimulating them to move into deeper water. Periwinkles are susceptible to flukes. Adult flatworms live in the gut of gulls and when the bird defecates eggs pass out too. Because the gulls roost on the upper shore the eggs may then be eaten by *L. rudis*. Larval flukes develop and if the periwinkle is eaten by gulls the cycle is completed. The periwinkle acts as a second host enabling the parasite to get back to the primary one.

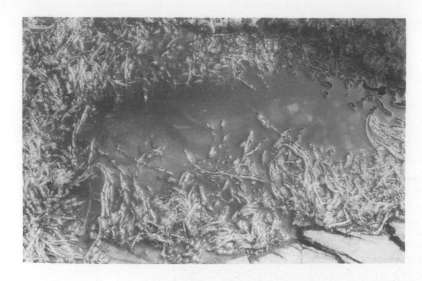

A rock pool of the upper shore
– an *Enteromorpha* pool

The brackish water prevents most algae from growing; only this green species can exist. Cloudy water is due to decayed seaweed which has been deposited by the tide.

A rock pool of the middle shore

1 *Lithothamnion*, a calcareous red alga, dominates the floor of the pool, it is tolerant of limpet grazing

2 *Corallina officinalis*, red alga, limited to fringes where there is no grazing by limpets

3 *Patella vulgata* (common limpet)

4 limpet with brown alga (*Scytosiphon*) growing on shell

5 *Scytosiphon lomentaria*, attached to *Fucus*

6 fragment of kelp washed in by the tide

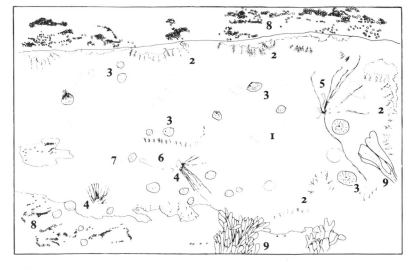

7 limpet scar

8 acorn barnacles

9 *Fucus* sp.

NB. the dark clumps are composites of red and brown algae that have escaped limpet grazing

A rock pool of the lower shore

1 *Laminaria digitata* (tangle)

2 *L. saccharina* (sugar kelp)

3 *Halidrys siliquosa* (sea oak)

4 *Rhodymenia pseudopalmata* (dulse)

5 *Cladophora rupestris*

6 *Lithothamnion* sp.

7 *Ascophyllum nodosum* (knotted wrack)

8 *Fucus serratus* (saw wrack)

ROCKPOOLS

When the tide goes out it will leave pockets of water trapped in hollows and depressions to produce distinct rockpool communities. For some species this will enable them to survive further up the shore; in spring it is possible to find *Laminaria* growing in the middle and upper shore, but high temperatures in summer will kill it. *Fucus serratus* can invariably be found in rock pools of the middle shore. Many organisms will use the pool for shelter as well as combating desiccation. However, not all the species discussed previously will be found in the pools, these pockets of still water exclude them. It may be that they are already specialised for their niche and life in the rockpool will require additional adaptations for survival. The limiting factors operating in a zone will not necessarily apply to the rockpools there and the difference will be represented by a different community. Deep rockpools will have their own vertical zonation. Over a period of several hours it is the condition of the static water which changes. Therefore, most of the limiting factors relate to the length of time it is standing before the tide returns.

THE LIMITING FACTORS

Temperature
: High air temperatures in summer heat the water and affect the dissolving of gases in water as well as increasing evaporation. In winter, upper shore rockpools may freeze.

Salinity
: Increased evaporation will cause the salinity to rise. Rain will dilute the seawater. Either will cause an osmotic problem with the organisms because few have the ability to regulate the body concentration. *Carcinus* is one of the exceptions.

Oxygen and pH
: The amount of dissolved oxygen varies with temperature and the degree of photosynthesis. In sunlight it is easy to see bubbles of oxygen on the fringe weeds. By late afternoon this slows down, stopping completely at night. The balance between respiration and photosynthesis also affects the carbon dioxide content. Carbon dioxide produces an acid in water and its addition and subtraction from the water changes the pH during 24 hours. Too much dissolved oxygen will slow down photosynthesis (the Warburg effect) and seaweeds high up will reach their peak by mid-morning. A decline in photosynthesis then occurs.

Organic matter
: Rockpools will trap dead and decaying organisms; seaweeds washed in from the lower shore often become caught. This attracts the scavenging animals. Shrimps are typically found here as are most of the detritus-eating crustacea.

ORGANISMS OF THE ROCK POOLS

Upper shore
: These pools will be dominated by *Enteromorpha* species as they are most tolerant of temperature extremes as well as ionic changes due to the lower salinity. *Pelvetia* is notably absent. *Carcinus* and *Leander* can both osmoregulate and may survive here.

Middle shore
: *F. serratus* may grow well here but few other lower shore species do. *Lithothamnion* and *Corallina* both grow, particularly if shaded. They may dominate and give their name to the type of pool. Many small, delicate species perform well in these pools e.g. *Ceramium, Nemalion, Scytosiphon*. The sides of the pools will have the most abundant growth (called fringe weed) because grazing limpets cannot climb the side. The floor will be grazed clear except for *Lithophyllum*. Small weeds will grow on the shells of the limpets – the only place where they will not be consumed. Shallow pools will be colonised by the snakeslock sea anemone. The green form of this anemone has a symbiotic dinoflagellate alga, *Symbiodinium* living in the cells. In bright sunshine the plant will be able to produce food for both. Barnacles are absent from rock pools, producing a clear dividing line near the edge. This may be due to problems with larval settlement or competition with the sheltered rock pool species.

Lower shore

With the displacement of organisms up the shore in these desiccation-free pools, sublittoral species will colonise the lower shore. 'Copses' of kelp live in the deeper ones with the much branched *Halidrys siliquosa*. This is aptly named sea oak as it has an abundance of animals that live amongst it. These pools may have echinoderms and octopuses which are more typical of offshore habitats.

PROBLEMS

Question 1

Dog-whelks are a common predator on other molluscs, especially mussels, limpets and barnacles. They are found on most rocky seashores and a gradual difference can be seen from shelter through to extreme wave action. The individuals in the photograph were collected from two different seashores (**A** and **B**) with varying degrees of wave action. The operculum is the opening through which the muscular foot emerges for attachment to the substrate.

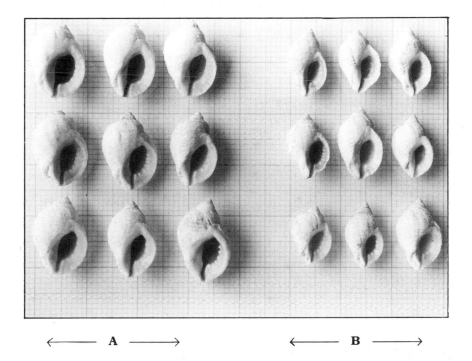

$\longleftarrow$ **A** $\longrightarrow$ $\qquad$ $\longleftarrow$ **B** $\longrightarrow$

a Measure the shell length and operculum length of each dog-whelk. (The smallest squares shown are 2 mm squares.) Produce a mean ratio of the two figures for each of the seashores. Could you represent the data graphically?

b Compare the ratios between the two seashores. Discuss the significance of the differences as adaptation to the wave action.

c Shell thickness varies considerably. Sheltered shores often have a higher incidence of thick shells. It does not appear to be an adaptation to wave action. Can you suggest a possible reason for this adaptation? Design an experiment to investigate your hypothesis.

The following data was obtained by analysis of gut content on a number of blennies over a year, from May to April. (Adapted from Qasim, 1957)

month	May	June	July	Aug	Sep	Oct	Nov	Dec	Jan	Feb	Mar	Apr
Barnacles	78	77	86	62	61	87	91	63	58	51	39	75
Amphipods	22	30	89	81	76	42	8	35	30	14	42	18
Isopods	17	18	73	56	39	19	29	17	23	26	18	10
Crabs	12	23	70	66	68	43	48	7	9	7	10	12
Fly maggots	–	–	–	6	4	6	6	18	15	13	8	–
Gastropods	34	18	55	47	22	56	47	44	40	27	34	41
Algae	83	70	31	43	47	40	39	85	47	49	61	62
Blenny eggs	2	5	–	–	–	–	–	–	–	–	–	–
% of individuals with empty guts	15	2	–	3	3	3	3	12	21	13	31	9

The figures are % occurence of different foods in the blenny guts

a Represent the data graphically.

b Which item is the most important prey for the blenny? Discuss the feeding pattern of this fish over the 12 months.

c What time of year do you think that the gut analysis of the blenny in the photograph was most likely to have been carried out? Use a hand lens if necessary to identify the gut contents.

d Where on the rocky shore does the fish obtain the maggots? What has happened in the environment to increase the maggots abundance?

e Blennies guard their eggs. What is the significance of the blenny eggs found in the gut in June?

f Whilst guarding eggs they must eat what is nearby. Can you find evidence of this in the data?

g Discuss the significance of the data for empty guts.

Question 3

Samples of similar size limpets (*Patella vulgata*) were collected from a rocky shore. They were taken from three areas: upper, middle and the lower shore. The radulae were removed and photographed.

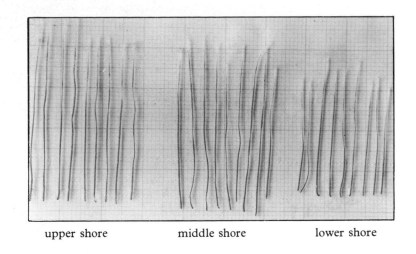

upper shore   middle shore   lower shore

a Measure the lengths of the radulae (the smallest squares are 2 mm squares). For each region of the shore give the mean length of radula. Calculate the standard deviation.

b Limpets only feed when they are covered by the tide. Produce a hypothesis to account for the differences between your calculated means.

c Can you devise an experiment to test your hypothesis?

Question 4

On the upper shore of a rocky beach four plots were marked out, each 20 m². A mark-recapture experiment was set up for the periwinkle, *Littorina rudis* and the following data recorded.

Plot	1	2	3	4
nos. marked (day 1)	198	150	240	123
total recaptured (day 2)	200	140	200	110
nos. marked recaptured	23	60	18	38

a Using the formula given on page 5, work out the density of periwinkles in each plot.

b Discuss and compare the densities of the four plots with regard to possible position on the beach and availability of food. What other factors will affect the population density?

c What problems may be encountered whilst performing the experiment?

d The length of gastropod shells are a good indication of age. When these periwinkles were marked the spire height was measured and the data recorded.

size /mm	1–2	3–4	5–6	7–9	9–10	11–12	13–14	15–16
frequency	34	48	74	263	138	56	86	4

Plot the data graphically. Discuss the age distribution of the organism. The data was collected towards the end of the long breeding season, late in the year. The data for the juveniles is surprisingly low. Can this be explained by experimental error?

PROJECTS

Besides the usual type of investigation on the rocky shore, such as a transect of communities to show zonation and the effects of wave action, a number of additional exercises can be rewarding.

1 Animal communities (epifauna) on the dominant seaweeds

Select several fresh samples of different seaweeds such as the fucoids, kelps and *Halidrys*. Vigorously wash each species separately in a bucket of seawater and identify the organisms which are dislodged. Compile a list for the different seaweeds and record the part of the plant to which they were attached (by washing each part separately). *Halidrys siliquosa* has a surprisingly large macrofauna living upon its fronds whilst *Laminaria digitata* has an extensive microcommunity within its domed holdfast. Some algae, e.g. *Ascophyllum*, have a poor epifauna. Construct food webs for the communities. If a record is made of the numbers of each animal species comprising the epifauna a pyramid of numbers can be constructed.

2 Epifauna of fringe weeds

Collect small samples of fringe weeds, e.g. *Ceramium*, *Halopitys* or *Corallina*, and keep them fresh in seawater until you are back in the lab. Put them in a petri dish of seawater and examine under a binocular microscope. The vast numbers of micro-organisms crawling and swimming around the fronds are quite amazing. For a detailed analysis, the fresh plant can be soaked in the dye Rose Bengal, made up in seawater. This helps remove the organisms and stains them pink. They can then be identified and counted.

3 Marking animals

Much can be learnt about animal movement by marking animals on the seashore. One of the commonest experiments is to mark a number of limpets with enamel paint and watch their progress over a period of days. By carefully removing them and placing them at different distances from their original sites, up to several metres away, the homing behaviour can be studied. Numbering crabs on the carapace can be used to measure their distribution patterns.

4 Plankton sampling

To complete any study of the seashore plankton samples should be examined. A large quantity of seawater needs to be filtered by a plankton net and although a small boat is ideal, a net can be hauled back and forth along the edge of a sea wall for 15 minutes. The samples should be allowed to settle for an hour in the dark and a pipette used to take up drops from the bottom. The best collections are made in the spring when the diatoms are in 'bloom'.

5 Rockpools

An interesting comparison can be made between rockpools selected in the different zones on the seashore. They can be mapped by placing a tape measure along one edge (the standard) and a second one at right angles. At intervals along the standard tape, measurements are recorded to the edges of the pool. Using a suitable scale it can then be drawn onto graph paper. On the pool outline a map of the vegetation and relative positions of animal grazers can be drawn. Temperature and oxygen readings should be taken at different times of the day. Attempt to relate approximate water volumes of the pools with the abundance of fauna, e.g. filter feeders.

6 Algal Desiccation

Examples of different algal species could be chosen from the littoral zones and weighed over a period of time and varying conditions, e.g. strong sunlight. Suitably graphed the changes can be related to the relevant position on the shore.

7 Pyramids of Biomass

By removing and weighing all organisms from a series of quadrat samples, productivity and community structure can be analysed in different zones.

3 — SAND AND MUD DEPOSITING SHORES

INTRODUCTION

Compared to the rocky shore, depositing shores look barren and devoid of life. At high tide when water movement is low, finely suspended particles rain down on to the shore. These depositing shores are moulded by different degrees of shelter to produce a range from clean, coarse sand (with few organisms) to muddy, bacteria-rich ones (with many organisms). In all cases shelter causes the material to settle and any movement, including water currents, will disturb the surface. Typically, the substrate is unstable. Any disturbance of the surface by water currents or occasional storms will affect the substrate and therefore the communities. Due to the very nature of their formation, depositing shores have little slope, hence the term mudflat.

Estuaries are typically sheltered shores where the velocity of the water has slowed to allow considerable deposition to occur. Substrates will be a mix of gravels, sands and fine silty mud. They occur where freshwater runs into the sea. The former is less dense, floating on the salty water. With changing tides, mixing gradually occurs.

THE SUBSTRATE

- particles may be of quartz, felspar or shell fragments
- particles are of an irregular shape, with pits and crevices; this gives a large surface area for the attachment of bacteria and microscopic algae (diatoms)
- between the particles (interstitial space) is a micro-community called the **meiofauna**, based on bacteria and diatoms
- mud particles are much smaller than those of sand, this gives a larger surface area with small interstitial spaces; the combination of both yields a richer community and a greater productivity
- the smaller interstitial space in mud means that water does not drain away and at low tide the surface of mudflats remains wet: communities living in the mud will not suffer from desiccation
- sandy shores do drain quickly so that upper shores suffer from desiccation, fewer species can survive
- water turbulence grades and sorts the particles so that many shores will show a transition from high water mark to low water e.g. shingle through sand to mud

Problems and features of living here

- no fixed substrate for attachment, except for the occasional stone on the upper shore
- some species are burrowers, requiring distinct forms of adaptation to live under the surface
- few producers are visible and the water is cloudy with silt and organic matter
- in very sheltered areas salt-marsh may develop
- depositing shores are typical of estuaries and here salinity changes daily; there are osmotic problems

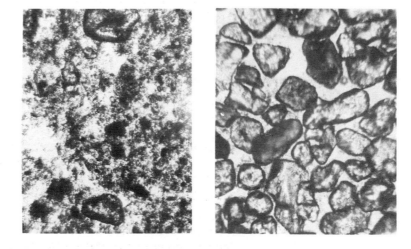

Left: substrate from an estuarine mudflat: note the small grain size and abundant detritus (there are two sand grains also present) (× 60)

Right: substrate from a sandy shore; note the large and relatively clean grains (× 60)

Precautions in fieldwork

Soft mud can be very dangerous and the danger increases towards the lower shore. Avoid soft mud and do not attempt to cross it.

Points of special interest

- a contrasting group of organisms to the rocky shore; good source of micro-organisms

DEPOSITING SHORE COMMUNITIES
animals of upper and middle sandy shores

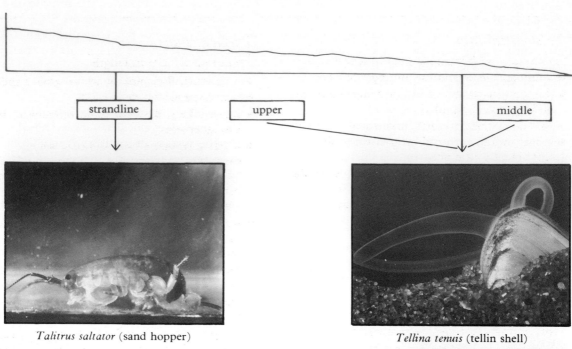

strandline

upper

middle

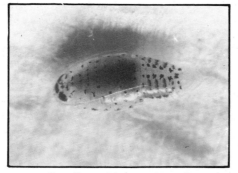

Talitrus saltator (sand hopper)

Tellina tenuis (tellin shell)

Arenicola marina (lugworm)

Cerastoderma edule
(common cockle)

Eurydice pulchra (an isopod)

Amphitrite johnstoni

PROBLEMS
- the surface dries at low tide; drainage occurs through sand
- the substrate is unstable
- no substrate for attachment
- no shelter, hence burrowing existence
- no seaweeds present for food

Talitrus saltator

(common sand hopper) 1.5 cm in length
- abundant on strandline amongst flotsam
- 'hopping' is achieved by releasing the flexed abdomen very rapidly
- feeds on organic debris, occasional predator
- it burrows in the sand on the upper shore leaving only at night
- cyclical migration from intertidal area to the strandline coincides with neap and spring tides to ensure feeding and immersion

Eurydice pulchra

an isopod crustacean 0.8 cm in length
- it has very long antennae and an oval body
- black, star-like chromatophores darken and lighten the body
- it burrows temporarily in sand at low tide, swimming vigorously with a rising tide
- it is a highly predaceous carnivore, with tearing mouthparts; digestion in a distensible hind gut may take up to 3 weeks

Arenicola marina

(lugworm) up to 20 cm in length
- lives at the bottom of a mucus lined 'U'-shaped burrow; a cast on the surface marks the tail end, a depression marks the head where sand is being engulfed
- organic matter is digested out of the sand and therefore clean, coarse sand will not support lugworms; tolerate low salinity
- sand is defecated at the surface every 45 minutes, this brings it into the wading birds' feeding zone; the abdomen is often eaten by curlews
- the tube is irrigated by body movements to oxygenate 13 pairs of red gills
- at low tide, atmospheric gas exchange takes place but it can survive anaerobically for 9 days
- small worms are common highest up the shore, migrating down with maturity; 2 year life span

Amphitrite johnstoni

a terebellid worm, 25 cm in length
- a sedentary worm with a tapering body
- it has 3 pairs of red gills and numerous tentacles which lie on the sand surface collecting detritus

Tellina tenuis

a tellin shell 2 cm in length
- a delicate, flat, pink or white, glossy shell
- it is common in clean sand
- it has a large foot for rapid burrowing as the tide goes out
- it has 2 separate long siphons; when burrowed, one enables it to draw in food like a vacuum cleaner from the surface, the other moves fluids in the other direction getting rid of waste
- water brings in detritus and oxygen; gills filter the detritus which is passed to the mouth for consumption
- the density of tellins is high in an area of sand and surface contact with the siphons may be the way that they space themselves to prevent intraspecific competition
- competition with a close relative, T. fabula, is avoided because T. tenuis lives at a higher level on the beach

Cerastoderma (Cardium) edule

common cockle shell
- it has a thick rounded shell, 3–5 cm in length, with distinct ribs and growth rings
- it is common in muddy sand and gravels
- the 2 siphons are very short and therefore it is restricted to living at the surface where it is susceptible to temperature variation
- it filters the water of suspended detritus
- the outlet siphon is narrow to produce more pressure, thus ensuring that waste is ejected away from the inlet water
- it spawns March – August, the larva lives in the plankton for 3 weeks and is often consumed accidently by parents
- it is tolerant of low salinity

ADDITIONAL SPECIES

Crangon vulgaris

(common shrimp) 5 cm in length
- it burrows quickly into sand by clearing it with the legs, peppered colouring by chromatophores gives good camouflage
- it preys on worms and is eaten by fish

See also *Nereis*, page 47.

DEPOSTING SHORE COMMUNITIES
animals of lower sandy shores

MIDDLE SHORE   LOWER SHORE   SUBLITTORAL

Cereus pedunculatus
(daisy anemone)

Crangon vulgaris (common shrimp)

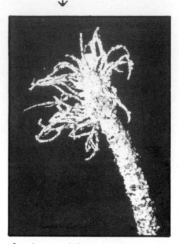

Lanice conchilega (sand mason)

Echinocardium cordatum (sea potato)

Corystes cassivelaunus (masked crab)

- no substrate for attachment or shelter
- burrowing existence necessary
- surf – lower region is the most prone to instability due to turbulence
- no seaweeds are present for food

SEA ANEMONES

Cereus pedunculatus

(daisy anemone) 3 cm in height

- it is pale, orange-buff coloured with a trumpet-shaped column; up to 700 tentacles
- buried in muddy sand, only the tentacles show at the surface; usually anchored below to a shell or stone
- it consumes depositing organic matter as well as crustaceans
- it is adaptable; found near entrance to estuaries and in rockpools
- *Peachia hastata* is a worm-like anemone and is capable of true burrowing as it does not attach to hard substrate; it has 12 tentacles;

Lanice conchilega

(sand mason worm) 20 cm in length

- it has a 35 cm tube, with distinct 4 cm showing above the sand, made from sand and shell fragments glued with mucus
- fine, pink, extensible tentacles collect food deposited by the tide
- *Owenia* is a worm producing a similar (but much finer) type of tube; *Owenia* can carry its tube around unlike *Lanice*

Nepthys hombergi

(catworm) 8–15 cm in length

- white, flattened muscular body with a dark line along the back; single thread at tail
- it is a carnivore with an eversible proboscis also used in burrowing
- has no permanent burrow, active swimmer
- it has slight tolerance to low salinity

Echinocardium cordatum

(sea-potato) 9 cm in length

- the deep (15 cm) burrow avoids the main effect of the turbulent surf at the surface
- behind the mouth are spade-like spines which are modified for digging
- the tube feet assist digging and produce mucus for lining the burrow; it is a deposit feeder
- the large, tube feet by the mouth collect sand grains which are cleaned of detritus
- the anus is at the top of the back and faeces are carried out of the burrow by a water current maintained by cilia

Corystes cassivelaunus

(masked crab) 4 cm in length

- it is a true burrowing crab (*Carcinus* can burrow for short periods)
- the long and very hairy antennae link to produce a tube, comparable with the siphons of bivalves
- water is drawn down the tube and under the carapace by the head, the reverse of that in other crabs; it forages for food at night

ADDITIONAL ANIMAL SPECIES

Ensis ensis

(common razor shell) 13 cm in length

- a long, narrow shellfish
- the siphons are very short and so it lives near the surface, the outlet siphon forces water out quickly ensuring that waste is blown clear of the inlet
- it is sensitive to surface vibration; it can burrow very quickly using the large muscular foot which can push as well as pull down into sand
- living in the surf is hazardous as it can easily be uncovered, reburrowing quickly is crucial; water is forced out of the mantle to soften the sand

Donax vittatus

(banded wedge shell) 3–4 cm in length

- variable colour (white-brown-purple) with a toothed edge to the shell on the inside
- a very active burrower, it survives on exposed beaches where it moves with the waves

Acronida brachiata (burrowing brittle star)

- the central disc is 1 cm in diameter with very long arms (16 cm)
- the arms are near the surface and can raise and lower the body; it is a detrital feeder

Haustorius arenarius

an amphipod, 1 cm in length

- it has a wedge-shaped body, (assists burrowing); nocturnal
- the eyes are indistinguishable; it is a filter feeder

PLANTS

Zostera sp. (eel grass) up to 1 m in height
see page 69

General view of an estuarine shore

- upper shore of gravel
  middle shore of gravel
  lower shore of mud flat

- brown seaweeds present as small clumps
- tall plants to the left are *Phragmites communis*
- foreground plant is sea club rush
- middle shore is covered by *Enteromorpha*

Typical animals of the estuary

Hydrobia ulvae (laver spire shell)

Scrobicularia plana (peppery furrow shell)

Corophium volutator (an isopod)

Carcinus maenas (common shore crab)

Nereis diversicolor (ragworm)

• minimal movement of water results in a deoxygenation of the substrate
• the abundance of bacteria and organic matter results in a sulphide layer i.e. a blackened mud, high in hydrogen sulphide
• variable salinity, changing during the course of the tides causing osmotic problems for the organisms
• mud is easier to burrow in than sand but more likely to collapse

---

GRAVELS

• give stability to the estuary edge, further supported by a small, developing salt-marsh
• larger pebbles are used by Fucoid algae for attachment
• only burrowers with thickened shells could live here e.g. cockle

SAND

• sand fills the spaces between the gravels and is home to a fauna of small worms and nematodes

MUD

• very soft mudflats dominate the shore
• the surface does not dry as drainage is poor and zonation across the shore is unlikely i.e. a lack of limiting factor gradient

Fucoid algae can grow if stones are present.

Fucus vesiculosus (bladder-wrack)

• it hybridises in variable salinity with other fucoids and the frond is narrow; it grows in a curly form

Fucus ceranoides

(the horned wrack) 70 cm in length

• characteristic of variable salinity; it has distinct forked tips on the frond

Nereis diversicolor

(ragworm) 6–9 cm in length

• a red line runs the length of the worm
• it is characteristic of estuaries, tolerating a low salinity; it can live high up on a sandy beach where freshwater is present
• it burrows temporarily at low tide
• it is omnivorous; it kills other worms; it secretes mucus into its burrow which traps organic matter for consumption
• spawns February–March; the female ruptures the body wall to release eggs (and dies); the larvae remain in adult burrows, avoiding the plankton; dispersal occurs later
• in more saline areas it is replaced by the King Rag *N. virens*, iridescent green
• ragworms are important prey for wading birds

Corophium volutator

(an amphipod) 0.5–0.9 cm in length

• it has a very large second pair of antennae which are used in locomotion
• the 5th pair of legs is used to anchor the animal in its 'U'-shaped burrow in the mud
• vast numbers are found on the mud ($12\,000\,m^{-2}$) as there is little interspecific competition
• it shows a tidal rhythm: rising to the surface with an incoming tide, swimming down on a receding tide, this helps it to maintain itself on the shore
• it crawls over the surface at low tide; the forelimb has a filter for collecting detritus
• it is a prime food source for the redshank

Scrobicularia plana

(peppery furrow shell) 6 cm in length

• it has a thin shell, often grey-black, stained by the sulphide in the mud
• it has very long, separate siphons for sucking up organic matter like a vacuum cleaner
• it is tolerant of low salinity but very susceptible to frost so it lives deep in the mud
• it occupies a very similar niche to *Macoma* (Baltic tellin) and much competition occurs

Hydrobia ulvae

(laver spire shell) 0.3–0.6 cm in length

• although small it may dominate the mud by its numbers: $9000\,m^{-2}$
• tolerant of low salinity; it is typical of estuaries
• it secretes a mucus raft which will carry it floating on the water surface: the tide disperses the raft across the mud, usually with its egg capsules
• its food varies from diatoms and detritus to bacteria on bare mud
• it is the principle food of the shelduck

Carcinus maenas (common shore crab)

• the only crab able to osmoregulate effectively

PLANTS

Estuarine fucoids

Fucus ceranoides is typical of brackish water and is the main brown alga of the estuary. However, no large seaweed is common on depositing shores because of the lack of a hard substrate for attachment and they are limited to large stones found in the upper areas of some shores. Where they do occur, periwinkles and crustaceans will take shelter under the fronds. Bladder- and spiral-wracks will grow in estuaries but take on a curled, twisted form. Hybridisation is commonplace making recognition difficult.

ANIMALS

Estuarine crabs

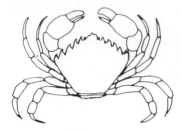

Carcinus maenas is the only British crab able to actively osmoregulate in dilute seawater, although in freshwater it soon dies. It regulates with antennal glands, small bladder-like organs at the base of the antennae. This allows the crab to penetrate far up the estuary, living in concentrations of only 0.6% salinity. This crab shows a seasonal movement; in summer it is common high on the shore moving down to survive the cold winters. Females carrying eggs move to the estuarine entrance. Hatching larvae are released into seawater with a higher chance of reaching the plankton of the sea.

ADDITIONAL SPECIES OF THE ESTUARINE SHORE

PLANTS

Diatoms

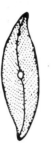

- *Pleurosigma* is a common diatom, it secretes a mucus coat to resist desiccation
- it may undergo daily migration to the mud surface in bright sunlight, a distance of about 3 mm, returning at night
- distribution in the estuary is determined by the salinity; for some, if the sulphide layer is too near the surface, their density is reduced, peak diatom 'blooms' are in the summer
- light reaching the mud is a problem if the water is cloudy
- *Euglena*, a common organism of the mud, develops distinct green patches on the surface, moving up in bright sunlight; this rhythm is linked with the tidal movement

Enteromorpha sp.

(a green alga) see page 15 for detail.
- in spring the estuarine mud surface is carpeted with it
- it is typical of a shore with variable salinities

ANIMALS

Microfauna

the microscopic animals which live in the spaces between the particles of mud and sand
- **ciliate** protozoans, including stalked forms, are abundant
- the tiny shells (<1 mm) are from Foraminifera protozoans, the shell is of calcium carbonate and chitin; they move and feed by pseudopodia; they consume diatoms and bacteria
- **nematodes** reach densities of 28 000 per 100 cm² of mud and are visible in mud as tiny white worms; they live in the top few centimetres of mud emerging at night, when environmental stress is minimal, to feed on bacteria and deposits
- **copepods** use thoracic appendages for swimming, living typically in the plankton; mud dwellers (<1 mm) are **harpacticoid** copepods

Lineus ruber (a nemertine worm) elongated flat worm, 10 cm in length
- it is a mud burrower emerging at night to feed on nematodes, captured with an eversible pharynx
- tolerates salinities down to 0.8% by covering its body in slime

Mya arenaria (sand gaper, although it lives mainly in mud) 15 cm in length

- it has a thin, soft shell for mud burrowing, may be stained black by sulphide layer; it is permanently burrowed
- the adult foot is greatly reduced and so it cannot reburrow if dug up; it is a suspension feeder
- as it grows it moves deeper, the siphons increasing in length to reach the surface; these are so long (up to 0.5 m) that they cannot be withdrawn into the shell; the siphons are joined

Crepidula fornicata (slipper limpet) 4 cm in length, introduced from America with oysters

- not a true limpet, it lives on most substrates; the base is attached to stone or shells making colonies
- it filter feeds and is the chief competitor with the oyster for food, hence, considered by some to be a serious pest
- it changes sex with age; males are small, females larger

Gammarids (amphipod crustaceans) the body is laterally compressed

- it is common under stones and weed but it can live out of water for short periods of time
- it can osmoregulate; the degree of osmoregulation affects distribution within the estuary causing zonation, page 52
- detrital feeders; **epizooites** attach to their bodies e.g. ciliates
- sex of the offspring is determined by water temperature, e.g. in *G. duebeni* below 5°C it is male, above 5°C, female

Neomysis (opossum shrimp) 1–2 cm in length
- an active swimmer in estuarine waters; it is abundant at the water edge of an incoming tide
- it feeds on organic debris, bacteria and diatoms; it falls prey to fish, especially flounder

Gasterosteus aculeatus (3-spined stickleback) 5 cm in length
- a freshwater fish which has adapted to salt water; the estuarine variety has 20–30 bony plates on the body flanks as an adaptation to the salt; freshwater types have only 4–5 plates
- it feeds on small crustaceans

Platichthys flesus (flounder) 30 cm in length
- the commonest estuarine flatfish, it is tolerant of very low salinity and is able to survive in rivers; the young feed and grow in estuaries, moving seaward to breed; impermeable scales stop water entry
- it feeds on a wide variety of crustaceans and polychaetes

Tadorna tadorna (shelduck) 60 cm in length red bill, green head, brown band on shoulders

- the bill has a fine filter along the edge, this enables mud to be sucked in at the front and squeezed out at the sides, retaining any organisms in the mouth; its chief diet is *Hydrobia*, a tiny snail, thousands will be eaten each day by each duck
- it nests on sand dunes in old rabbit burrows

See also *Elminius*, *Littorina littorea*, oystercatcher and *Mytilus*.

ORGANISMS ON DEPOSITING SHORES

GENERAL FEATURES

- the sediment necessitates burrowing which requires many adaptations to obtain nutrients and oxygen from the outside
- productivity on the shore is poor, organisms require nutrients, most of which comes from the sea or up river
- bacteria are important producers here and large plants are absent
- the communities are dominated by animals
- 3 types of community identified: microflora, microfauna and macrofauna
- zonation of communities down the shore not as marked as rocky shores
- zonation of organisms does occur along an estuary
- much overlap between the types of depositing shores: stones, sand, mud

SUMMARY OF THE LIMITING FACTORS AFFECTING ORGANISMS

Shore type	Very coarse sandy shore	Fine sandy shore	Muddy shore
Turbulence	high	average – low	very slight
Particle size	> 2 mm	0.2–0.002 mm	< 0.002 mm
Slope	steep	gradual	flat
Water content	low	variable	high
Drying out	rapid	slow	negligible
Oxygen level	high	low	deoxygenated
Sulphide layer	absent	slight	present
Amount of organic detritus	slight	variable	high causing dark colour of mud
Number of macro-organisms	low – absent	variable	high

- **Turbulence:** this sorts the particles so that the greater the wave action the coarser the material deposited on the beach. Sand is more unstable than mud. Waves tend to clear the sand of organic matter. Severe gales may remove sand and in calmer months redeposit it.
- **Slope:** the gradient is proportional to the particle size; shingle creates steep banks and silt creates mudflats.
- **Water content:** this too is affected by the size of particles. Mud draws water up by capillarity at low tide. Coarse sands have large air spaces and so drainage is rapid.
- **Aspect:** south facing shores are most likely to dry out, any shade will slow this down as well as giving protection from drying wind.
- **Oxygen and sulphide layer:** oxygen diffuses into the substrate from water and the air. Bacteria feed on organic matter and release hydrogen sulphide; without oxygen this produces ferrous sulphide, giving black sand. With oxygen an oxide, similar in colour to clean sand, develops; this is the pale, oxidising layer at the surface.

- **Temperature:** high air temperatures will affect drying and kill microfauna at the surface of mud which are usually unaffected by desiccation. In winter interstitial water may freeze, causing a high mortality rate. This is especially so in estuaries where the salinity is lower and the freezing point not so depressed. However, some organisms are quick to recolonise, particularly polychaetes. Bivalves are much slower to recolonise. Temperature becomes more constant with depth, to avoid extremes microfauna can migrate away from the surface.
- **Salinity:** rain on the shore can affect the microfauna in the interstitial spaces. Macrofauna will burrow deeper. Salinity is more variable on these types of shore than others and animals either conform, regulate or move away. Avoidance of freshwater is the common feature: *Inachus*, a spider crab, moves into deeper water; *Nereis* burrows and tolerates the absorption of water by its tissues. *Carcinus* and certain other kinds of crustacean can osmoregulate.

ZONATION ON DEPOSITING SHORES

Three forms of zonation can be distinguished:
- horizontal
- vertical (micro and macrofauna)
- distribution along estuaries

HORIZONTAL ZONATION

Although poorly defined, zonation does occur here. Sieving sand at several points down a sandy shore will give a horizontal distribution of species from the strandline to the sublittoral region. The gradual slope ensures that the community boundaries are not obvious because the transition between limiting factors is less marked. The transition from minimum to maximum within a factor is also gradual. Also, the ability to burrow helps the organism to avoid changes on the surface. Where the substrate shows a change from gravel near the top, through sand to mud further down a more noticeable fluctuation in communities will be seen. For example, the thicker shelled Venus bivalves are needed for burrowing in coarse material; the Gapers are thinner shelled and limited to finer substrates.

Mud does not drain at low tide, the fine material holds the water by capillarity. One of the major limiting factors in causing zonation on seashores (desiccation) does not apply here and as a consequence zonation is almost imperceptible. The upper region of sandy shores does, however, drain as the particles are much larger than mud. There are few species here. Fig. 10 shows the results of a transect across a sandy shore. The small amphipod crustacean, *Talitrus*, lives most of the day burrowed in the sand near the strandline and emerging at night to feed on organic matter washed up by the sea. Numbers of *Nereis* peak in the upper shore where freshwater run off reduces the salinity. The lugworm, *Arenicola*, is the dominant animal in stable sand, on mud shores its burrow will collapse. There is a marked difference in age range, those near the top of the shore are youngest (see Fig. 11). A comparison of transects on sand and rocky shore is fascinating as it introduces both similar and dissimilar aspects of limiting factors as well as analogies between niches, e.g. *Talitrus* and *Ligia*.

VERTICAL ZONATION

Macrofauna The larger organisms burrow within the sediment giving a vertical zonation (see Fig. 14). All are dependent upon the surface for their oxygen, food and possibly gametes. This distribution reduces competition for space, younger individuals are often nearer the surface. The sand gaper, *Mya*, moves deeper with age. If dug up it cannot reburrow.

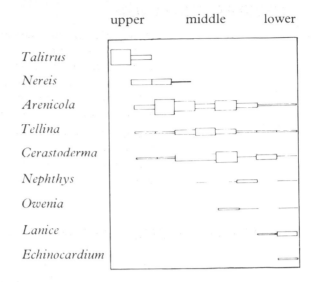

Fig. 10 Results of a transect on a sandy shore; samples of sand were dug and sieved at 40 m intervals

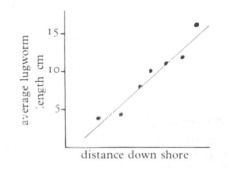

Fig. 11 The age distribution of lugworms on a sandy shore

Microfauna On a sandy beach ripples form, this represents a microscopic sorting of the sediment and it affects the microfauna. Many concregate in the trough, where the finer particles are present and water collects. The top of the trough is coarse material which dries out. The depth to which they will survive depends on the depth of the oxidising layer, i.e. the depth of oxygen availability. Only anaerobic organisms will enter the sulphide layer. The surface is alkaline, changing with depth to acidic. Environmental stress does not develop gradually through the surface but suddenly. The microfauna is limited to a range of a few centimetres, the exact depth changes diurnally as they migrate. Most interstitial animals live close to their lethal limit.

ESTUARINE ZONATION

Estuaries are regions of semi-enclosed water where the rivers enter the sea. As the tide flows inland the denser seawater flows along the bottom with the freshwater flowing over the top and gradual mixing occurs. This is affected by the width and depth of the estuary such that a strong pressure of river water may cause dilution and so reduce the salinity considerably. The usual result is a gradation of salinity along the length of the estuary. This influences the distribution of some estuarine organisms. See the diagram below.

Zonation invariably occurs across the estuary. Wind action at the surface increases turbulence which, in turn, affects sediment deposition. The sheltered side of the estuary develops a salt-marsh; the opposite bank is an assortment of mud, sand and shingle. This will be present if the estuary is wide enough for the wind to 'whip' up the surface.

DISTRIBUTION OF ANIMALS ALONG AN ESTUARY

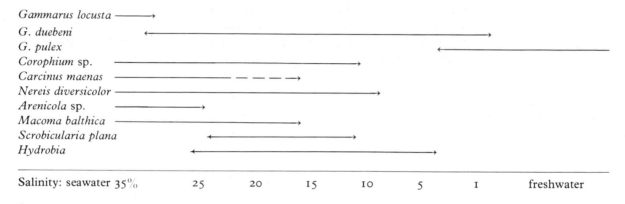

THE BURROWING NICHE

Two principal difficulties face animals when burrowing:
- entering the surface and
- digging within the substrate.

Both will be influenced by the grain size. Soft mud is easy to displace but the walls of the burrow will just as easily collapse. *Nereis* lines the walls of temporary burrows with mucus to strengthen them whilst lugworms restrict their niche to sand making permanent burrows. Bivalves require harder and thicker shells according to the hardness of the substrate, e.g. cockles are found amongst gravel, peppery furrow shells are found with their thin shells in mud. Bivalves begin to dig by probing forward with the foot; the shell muscles contract quickly, forcing water on to the substrate like a water pistol to blow the sand away and soften it. Blood is forced into the tip of the foot, causing it to widen like an anchor. Muscles contract to bring the body down, rocking from side to side.

Worms are similar, but instead of blowing water they tap the substrate which draws water to the surface and softens it. Penetration is by the eversible pharynx.

Some animals, e.g. sand gaper and lugworm, remain burrowed all their lives. Although this avoids much of the environmental stress found at the surface it does present certain problems.

PROBLEMS OF A BURROWED EXISTENCE

The chief problems are those of communication with the surface:
- obtaining oxygen
- obtaining food
- finding a mate

Oxygenated water can be drawn down by legs in *Corophium* or body movement in the worms. Bivalves use siphons with a current created by cilia. Food is considered in the next section. Many animals shed gametes into the burrow and water currents carry them out, but this requires synchronisation so that all the animals spawn together. Low temperatures stimulate lugworms; high temperatures affect sand gapers. The state of the tide is important in order to prevent the young from being washed away; many are lost at low tide.

FEEDING RELATIONSHIPS ON DEPOSITING SHORES

The apparent barrenness of these shores suggests that the source of energy is like few other ecosystems. Organic matter, washed in by the tide and washed down by rivers, accumulates amongst the sediment. Bacteria may live on this but they also represent vital food producers, because they exhibit photosynthesis and **chemosynthesis**. Two nutritional types exist

- **photoautotrophic** sulphur bacteria exist in the surface, photosynthesising but using H_2S as a hydrogen donor to reduce CO_2
- **chemoautotrophic** sulphur bacteria exist in the sulphide layer, they oxidise H_2S and chemical energy is released, substituting for light.

With an unsurpassed reproductive rate, bacteria productivity can be very high on muddy shores.

The food sources available to herbivorous animals in this ecosystem are

- bacteria
- microalgae, e.g. diatoms, *Euglena*
- macroalgae, e.g. *Fucus, Enteromorpha, Ulva*
- organic matter, including the strandline
- salt-marsh, an important source of organic matter (dealt with separately in the next chapter)

Fig. 12 A simplified food web of a sandy shore

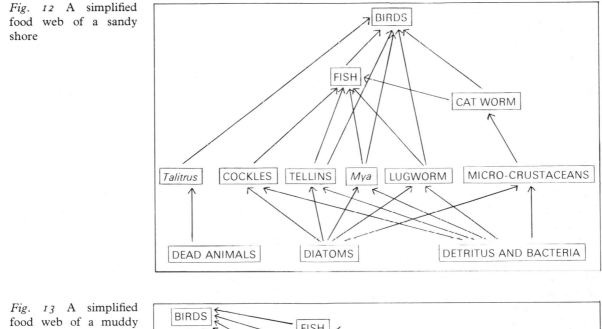

Fig. 13 A simplified food web of a muddy shore

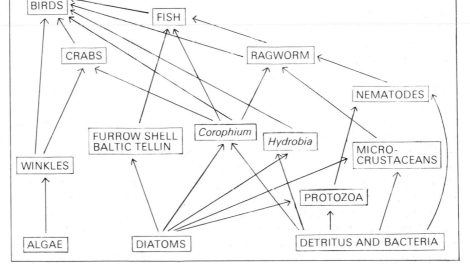

FAECAL SOUP

From the food webs it can be seen that surface bacteria are consumed by a high proportion of the animals. Most ingest large quantities of organic matter, which is stripped of the micro-organisms, and defecated back onto the surface. Thus the surface is a soup of faeces in which the micro-organisms breed. Recycling takes about three days. *Hydrobia*, a tiny snail found in densities of millions, can avoid reconsuming their faeces for up to twelve days, which allows the perfect broth to develop! Some faeces are nutritionally ideal immediately. Oyster faeces are eaten directly by *Nereis virens* and *Corophium*.

COMPETITION

Living on depositing shores is highly specialised and the diversity of species is less than on the rocky shore where productivity is higher. Those animals that have adapted to live amongst sediment have relatively few competitors. On the rocky shore a host of gastropod molluscs like periwinkles, top shells and limpets compete with each other; here, *Hydrobia* is the dominant gastropod. Interspecific competition is therefore limited whilst intraspecific competition is an important factor. Predation is the main factor in limiting density but densities are very high e.g. *Hydrobia* lives in densities of 9 000 and *Corophium* 12 000 per square metre.

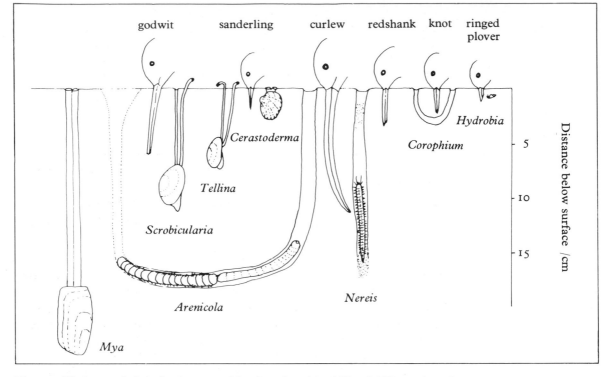

Fig. 14 Waders and their food: competition is reduced by bills of different lengths (after Green, 1968)

BIRDS OF DEPOSITING SHORES

Waders are the birds most commonly associated with these shores and their numbers can reach huge figures; in the Ribble, Morecambe and Dee estuaries in England as many as a million waders a year are accommodated. Estuaries are essential feeding grounds for these birds on their winter migrations. Birds vary their diet according to the abundancy and size of the prey. In addition, redshank selection depends on temperature: it switches from *Corophium* to *Macoma* and *Nereis* below 5°C. The end of the winter is when prey is at its least dense but at its maximum size. Waders feed, throughout the year, at night as well as by day, their feeding rhythm governed by the tides. Night feeding uses tactile senses. The bill is very sensitive and those which are very long, e.g. curlew, have a prehensile tip which opens under the mud. Interspecific competition can be reduced in two ways. Waders with different bills go for different items. Secondly, competition for the same prey may be avoided by age selection, e.g. oystercatchers take three-year-old mussels, eiders take only young ones. Intraspecific competition is avoided by territorial spacing, e.g. as in herons.

PROBLEMS

Question 1

You will probably find an 'A' level textbook useful to help you answer this question. Polychaetes living in the intertidal sediments need respiratory pigments because of the low oxygen tension. The haemoglobin differs considerably between species and this is reflected in its properties. The data below is for the catworm, which has haemoglobin in its coelom as well as in the blood, and the lugworm. (From Jones, 1954 and Prosser and Brown, 1961)

| % saturation | Catworm (*Nepthys hombergi*) | | | | Lugworm (*Arenicola marina*) |
| | Oxygen tension of vascular haem. | | Oxygen tension of coelomic haem. | | Oxygen tension of haemoglobin |
	pH 7.0	pH 7.4	pH 7.0	pH 7.4	
10	1.2	0.8	0.7	1.3	2.2
20	2.6	1.9	1.7	2.3	3.1
30	3.8	3.0	2.4	3.8	4.0
40	4.7	3.9	3.9	5.7	4.4
50	6.0	5.0	5.1	8.0	5.3
60	8.1	6.6	7.9	11.0	6.0
70	11.0	9.0	10.3	15.0	6.7
80	14.2	12.0	14.2	20.6	8.0
90	–	–	–	11.2

a Plot a graph to show the respective oxygen dissociation curves for the different species.

b How do these curves compare to human respiratory pigment?

c Compare the curves for the two species. What does this tell you about their affinity with oxygen?

d Why is pH an important consideration?

e In the catworm vascular haemoglobin exhibits the Bohr effect whilst that in the coelom shows the reverse. Suggest a possible reason for this.

f During an ebb tide the oxygen level of the water in the sediment falls. For the catworm it means the start of anaerobic respiration but not for the lugworm. In addition the lugworm will be found at a much higher level on the shore. With reference to the life style as well as the above data explain how the lugworm can delay anaerobic respiration for a considerably longer period.

Question 2

The two graphs show the particle size frequency (% volume) of (i) mineral particles and (ii) diatoms ingested by *Corophium volutator* and *Hydrobia ulvae*. Both diatoms and bacteria will be digested from the sediment before it is voided as faeces.

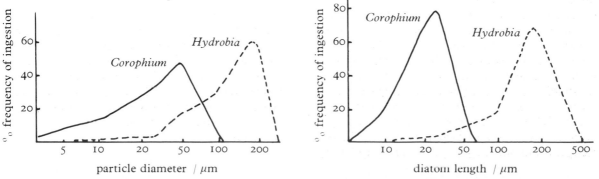

A Mineral particles

B Diatoms

a Discuss the interaction between the two species in sediments.

b Diatoms are more abundant on sand whilst bacteria are more abundant on silt. How does this affect the diet of the two species?

c Particle size selection in *Hydrobia* depends on the size of the snail. How does this affect your answers to **a** and **b**? Can you suggest any ways in which *Hydrobia* could be adapted to reduce the problems this causes?

PROJECTS

1 Transects of macrofauna A transect across a depositing shore is rewarding but requires different sampling equipment from rocky shores. At intervals of between 10 and 30 metres, depending on the slope (more frequent samples on steeper slopes), samples of the sediment are removed and sieved. It is best to use a coarse mesh to allow the sand to pass through but to retain the polychaete worms. To keep the samples uniform a large biscuit tin could be inverted and pressed into the sediment. The sample is dropped into the sieve and taken to water (pool or the sea) to be shaken. Species and density should be recorded. Ideally, a number of samples should be taken at each sample point on the transect line.

The macrofauna can be related to the particle size as well as the position on the shore. A small sample of the sediment at each sample station could be returned to the lab to try and relate particle size to different communities. Each sample is washed in freshwater to remove salt and organic matter. It is then dried and put through a nest of soil sieves to determine the percentages of the different particle sizes.

2 Shell thickness Either from the transect or from random samples on different depositing shores, the mean shell thickness for different bivalve species can be related to the particle size of the sediment.

3 Diatoms Always take small surface samples of the sediment back with you to look at under the microscope. Estuarine mud is especially good for examining diatoms. Work out a method of estimating the density of the different species. The density can be measured over a period of 24 hours and even over a number of months to see the diatom 'blooms'.

4 Meiofauna Just looking at a surface sample under the microscope will display the enormous variety of species present in the interstitial spaces. To extract the animals and estimate species density requires a modification of the Baermann funnel used in soil studies. A simplified technique is to use a piece of plastic drain piping with a very fine nylon mesh fixed over the end. The sediment is placed to a depth of about 8 cm and cotton wool packed on top. Then ice, made from filtered seawater, is packed on top of the wool. The organisms move away from the cold and if the bottom of the pipe is suspended in fresh seawater the organisms can be collected over several hours.

Alternatively, the sediment is mixed in a solution of seawater and Rose Bengal. This pink dye will stain the organisms so that they can be clearly seen. Again, comparisons of richness and diversity can be made between the different depositing shores.

5 Estuaries and salinity Salinity changes can be sampled along the length of an estuary. Because of the tidal variation this could be carried out at different stages of the tide during the day. If a boat is available samples can be taken across the estuary and at different depths so that a profile can be built up.

A transect from the sea to freshwater along the estuary length can be used to relate changes in the fauna and flora to the salinity variation. The animals that live in the estuary are a mixture of species that have adapted from habitats in the sea, land or freshwater. Try to determine the habitat origins of the organisms in the samples.

4 _____ SALT-MARSHES _____

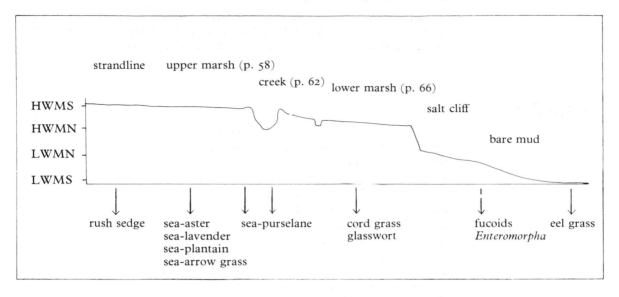

Fig. 15 A profile across the salt-marsh habitat

SALT-MARSH FORMATION

- sediment settles and builds up (accretion) in sheltered coastal areas
- vegetation colonises this mud, showing successive stages, to produce a mature marsh of specialised plants
- typical areas of development will be where shelter is afforded by shingle spits e.g. Blakeney, Norfolk in England, barrier islands lying just offshore e.g. Scolt Head, Norfolk in England, and along the banks of estuaries; in the latter cases strong currents and low salinity are also factors
- as plants begin to grow on the mud so they reduce water movement, further increasing accretion; rate of build up depends on the degree of shelter and the stability of the mud; vegetation will stabilise the substrate, their roots trapping and holding sediment
- colonisation and growth mainly occurs above the mean high water mark
- below the marsh a small cliff may occur due to erosion by tidal currents; the existence and height will vary according to the degree of erosion
- the soil which develops below the marsh is a gley type, that is, based on alluvial material; it is high in nutrients and has been cultivated by man where waterlogging has been prevented, e.g. by building a sea wall

PROBLEMS AND FEATURES

- the marsh is flooded and waterlogged by the tides, the relative flatness means that drainage is slow after flooding

- the soil (sediment) has a very high salt content which decreases towards the upper shore
- With so much salt in the soil, obtaining water by vascular plants will be almost impossible. Algae absorb water through their entire surface; vascular plants obtain it through the roots. If the soil has a higher salt concentration than the plant then water will pass from the root to the mud. **Halophytes** are plants that are highly specialised to tolerate the salt and ensure that the concentration gradient is in their favour.
- salt may accumulate in patches to produce an area of the marsh completely devoid of any plants called **salt pans**
- differential adaptation by plants to salt may lead to zonation across the salt-marsh
- oxygenation of the mud is very low, plants must obtain this from the air in special tissue
- creeks dissect the marsh and are unstable
- there is a poor diversity of fauna; many originate from terrestrial species

SPECIAL POINTS OF INTEREST

- zonation, showing colonisation and succession
- plants show structural and physiological adaptations e.g. salt glands, C_4 photosynthesis
- algae can exist in unattached forms: **ecads**

1 *Armeria maritima*
(thrift)

2 *Juncus maritimus*
(sea-rush)

3 *Limonium vulgare*
(sea-lavender)

4 *Plantago maritima*
(sea-plantain)

5 *Halimione
portulacoides* (sea-
purselane)

6 *Spergularia marina*
(sea-spurrey)

- partial flooding during spring tides causes a drag which uproots plants
- low salt content in the soil (sediment)
- shows a transition from salt-marsh to dry land
- strandline at the top of this region has deposits of organic matter and quantities of inorganic flotsam, e.g. plastic bottles, which have a shading effect on the plants
- the most stable and constant habitat in the salt-marsh

STRANDLINE SPECIES

Juncus maritimus (the sea-rush)

- tufts up to 60 cm make this a distinct band
- it grows on the high water spring tide mark
- it has a long, tubular, bright green leaf
- dense tufts shade the ground below slowing down evaporation, thus this region may be wetter than lower down the shore, allowing middle marsh species to grow here
- floating seaweed becomes entangled around the base encouraging stabilisation and growth of diatoms and blue-green algae
- it is not tolerant of a high salt content
- the seeds develop only in freshwater; they can germinate under anaerobic conditions
- in estuaries, where salinities are lower, it is replaced by *Phragmites*, (see page 68)

THE UPPER MARSH

Aster tripolium (the sea-aster)

- there are several growth forms, depending on the salinity, from a stunted 5 cm in height to 180 cm types in optimum conditions
- a short lived perennial with pale purple flowers produced in mid summer
- it can be found throughout the marsh but the seeds require freshwater for germination
- seed dispersal by wind is impeded as the fruits tend to clump together and fall to the ground; tidal water flooding the marsh then disperses them, this helps to prevent loss of seeds to the land
- it is intolerant of shade
- the leaves are often consumed by wildfowl

Plantago maritima (the sea-plantain)

- the narrow leaves offer less resistance to water flow when immersed
- it produces very dense roots
- it is common in upper and middle marsh
- shows great tolerance to a variety of stresses, forms part of several different communities e.g. mountains and moorland

Limonium vulgare (the sea-lavender)

- a short, woody perennial, about 12 cm high
- lanceolate leaves combined with its small size, offers least drag in water amongst the plants here
- it has a deep tap root
- it has broad lavender-like flowers which can colour the salt-marsh purple
- salt glands are found on the underside of the epidermis, excreting excess salt from the cell sap, up to 0.5 mm^3 of salt per hour; it is the most salt-tolerant species in the upper marsh
- approximately 20% of the root is air space, to overcome the absence of oxygen in the partly waterlogged soil
- chloroplasts in the cells are known to accumulate salt and may be involved in creating a medium suitable for modified photosynthesis

Cochlearia officinalis (scurvy grass)

- up to 50 cm in height
- not a grass but a member of the cabbage family
- the leaves are heart shaped and succulent; it has white flowers; it is normally found on drier patches
- succulence is caused by an uptake of water to compensate for the intake of salt
- an aphid, *Lipaphis cochleariae*, and a bettle, *Phaedon cochleariae*, feed specifically on this plant

ADDITIONAL PLANT SPECIES OF THE SALT-MARSH

Glaux maritima (sea-milkwort)

- a short, creeping perennial
- it is able to tolerate low light levels as a shade plant
- adult plants tolerate high salinity
- salt glands excrete salt from the leaves
- in drier conditions it will form the basis of a community

Atriplex hastata (orache)

- it is often found amongst strandline debris where the nitrogen content is high; the seeds float and are dispersed by the tide

STRANDLINE AND UPPER MARSH

ADDITIONAL SPECIES

Armeria maritima

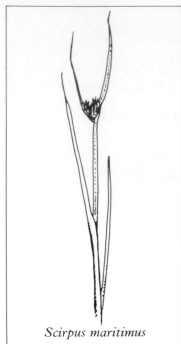

Scirpus maritimus

(thrift, see also pages 9 and 95)

- a common stress-tolerant plant able to cope with most maritime habitats e.g. the splash zone of rocky shore
- it may form a dominant band of vegetation on the upper marsh where its pink flower colours the marsh in early summer
- salt glands for excreting salt are present on the leaves and it is therefore tolerant of high salt content
- it is tolerant of grazing and this may be the reason for its abundance on some salt-marshes
- a deep root system, where food storage occurs, gives it an added advantage of resistance over other competitors in the marsh
- its narrow leaves and squat nature avoids water current drag

See also *Scirpus* (sea club-rush, page 46) and *Festuca* (page 81).

SUMMARY OF ADAPTATIONS ASSISTING VASCULAR PLANTS IN THE SALT-MARSH
- salt glands
- they have narrow leaves and are low growing to reduce surface area in contact with flowing water
- large air spaces in the stem bring air down from the leaves to the roots to counteract waterlogging

TRANSITION TO A FRESHWATER MARSH

In some places, especially in areas of high rainfall, notably Scotland, Ireland and parts of Wales, the strandline may mark a transition into a freshwater bog. *Carex* (sedges) will be common amongst the *Juncus* and this gives way to *Scirpus maritimus*, the sea club rush. The latter is a good indicator of very low salinity and may also be found on salt-marshes high up the estuary where it merges with *Phragmites communis*, the common reed (page 68). In Scotland and Scandinavia the common flag iris may replace the *Juncus*.

ALGAE

As well as diatoms growing in the upper surface of the sediment, several species of larger algae can be found wrapped around the stems of the salt-marsh plants. Many are just broken fragments of seaweed washed in by the tide but some use the tide for dispersal e.g. *Enteromorpha*. Becoming entangled in the marsh can be an advantage as it is increases stability. The large fucoid algae grow here in unattached forms, the stems of the vascular plants preventing them from being washed away. Light for photosynthesis could be a problem living amongst the tall marsh plants. Many algal species have growth peaks when the tall salt-marsh plants do not shade them out, e.g. *Ulothrix* is an alga that grows prolifically in spring, a time when marsh plants are only beginning to grow. Alternatively, algae may grow as epiphytes; green threads of *Enteromorpha nana* attach to *Juncus*.

ANIMALS OF THE SALT-MARSH

Tubifex

an oligochaete worm 1 cm in length

- it lives in the top layer of sediment; wriggling movements help to aerate the burrow; it may be present in huge numbers reddening the surface

Most of the animals of the upper marsh are terrestrial arthropods which have adapted to live in a habitat that floods daily.

Saldula palustris

(salt-marsh bug) 0.4 cm in length
- a dark head and thorax gives the bug good camouflage against the mud; mostly found in the drier parts of the marsh
- it is an active predator on other insects living here
- it can survive prolonged periods of immersion in seawater, where it continues to be active
- the young nymphs move on to the lower shore and can be seen running over mud in search of flies caught in the surface film
- the Saldidae family has several seashore species

Aphid

(the root aphid)
- several species of aphid are found on the upper marsh; this one is found on *Aster* roots; flooding restricts it to well drained places

Dicheirotrichus gustavii

(carabid beetle)
- a voracious carnivore coming out at night to feed on insects and crustaceans, e.g. *Gammarus*, *Corophium*
- during flooding by spring tides they remain in their burrows at night

Phaedon cochleariae

(a Chrysomelid beetle) 3 mm in length
- a bright blue beetle feeding on *Cochlearia*
- the name is derived from the fact that this genus of beetle is a common pest of oil-seed rape
- it falls prey (particularly the larvae) to carnivorous beetles

Anurida maritima

(marine springtail) see also page 15
- it has a circadian rhythm following the tide; it emerges from a burrow shortly after the tide retreats
- its greatest density occurs where the vegetation is relatively thin e.g. near pools of standing water
- higher up the salt-marsh, where the vegetation cover is thicker, competition with more terrestrial springtails restrict its distribution

Lycosa purbeckensis

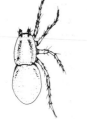

(wolf spider) 0.9 mm in length
- it is very dark brown with some lighter patches on the carapace; small white dots are seen on the abdomen
- it runs rapidly over the surface of mud, feeding on beetles, bugs and small crustaceans
- due to the flat gradient of the salt-marsh, the tide rises too fast for the spider to return to the strandline; it dives to the base of the vegetation where it stays with a trapped air bubble for up to several hours

Birds

due to flooding only a few species of birds attempt to nest on salt-marshes
- skylarks and meadow pipits nest on the raised areas
- yellow wagtail and lapwing nest on grazed, higher marshland
- redshanks nest on the edges of the creeks
- shelduck, along with the above, regularly feed on the marsh

See also *Littorinids*, *Hydrobia*, *Carcinus*, *Corophium* and *Orchestia*.

1 *Halimione portulacoides* (sea-purselane)

2 *Puccinellia maritima* (common salt-marsh grass)

3 *Spartina* sp. (cord grass)

4 stones remaining after tidal scouring

5 bank coated in *Vaucheria*

PROBLEMS and FEATURES

- the edges of the creek are unstable due to erosion; the ebb and flood of the tide with sediment scours the borders of the creeks twice a day
- slumping of the edge will cause a step arrangement; if the mud is not washed away it may be recolonised by salt-marsh species
- daily scouring by the tide will prevent vascular plants growing on the steep sides
- the tops of the edges are raised, being higher than the salt-marsh; this is called the levee
- drainage at the edge is high; obtaining water is a problem for organisms
- salt concentrations in the mud are high
- if the creek is blocked a deep pool or **channel pan** develops
- creeks make up almost a quarter of the area of a salt-marsh

---

Halimione portulacoides

(sea-purselane)

- a low growing, bushy plant with elliptical leaves
- a characteristic species of the creek banks, where drainage is greatest
- sediment becomes trapped between lateral branches of the woody stems that lay prostrate and so adds to the accretion
- the leaves have a dense pile of velvet-like hairs which help to reduce water loss by transpiration (the soil here is the least waterlogged part of the salt-marsh)
- extensive woody rhizomes grow deep into the banks, giving some stability and resistance to the scouring water in the creek
- it is intolerant of grazing
- it may be affected by low temperatures in winter; it is rarely found in Scotland or Scandinavia
- an epiphytic red alga *Bostrychia scorpioides* attaches to the base of the stem, obtaining shelter in the mud
- several fungi (moulds) are associated with the root system, forming mycorrhizae; this may help the plant to obtain sufficient nutrients in a well drained soil
- it is susceptible to oil pollution
- it is a refuge for many salt-marsh insects and spiders

Puccinellia maritima

(common salt-marsh grass)

- grows to a height of 80 cm
- it is found between the sea-purselane and *Spartina* zones; it merges in with upper marsh species
- it is a shallow-rooted plant which may colonise bare mud

- it produces long runners which trap sediment thus speeding up stabilisation
- seeds can be produced without fertilisation
- fungi on the roots develop mycorrhizae which help the plant to obtain sufficient nutrients in a well drained soil
- it produces fine tussocks which can be colonised by invertebrates; spiders and mites are especially abundant
- the leaves may roll to cover the stomata, slowing transpiration and conserving water
- it produces a canopy of leaves early in the spring and will shade out other species such as *Spartina*

ADDITIONAL PLANT SPECIES

Festuca rubra

(red fescue) (see also page 81)

- a fine hair-like grass often found near the base of the common salt-marsh grass
- it is salt tolerant
- it is very tolerant of grazing and under such conditions may become dominant with *Armeria*

Vaucheria sp.

- a brown filamentous alga
- it is a tiny alga which may grow in such profusion that it produces a thick, conspicuous layer on the mud surface with an appearance like felt
- it colonises the steep sides of the creeks, where vascular plants are unable to attach, by using rhizoids
- it secretes a mucilage which binds the mud surface; mucilage reduces water loss from the cells
- *Calothrix* and other blue-green algae may be associated with *Vaucheria*

SALT-MARSH CREEKS

Creeks are a characteristic feature of salt-marshes forming during the early stages of marsh development. They ramify across surface and may occupy over a quarter of the area. Continual scouring by the tides will maintain them and the steep sides makes it difficult to walk across them.

Aerial view of a salt-marsh

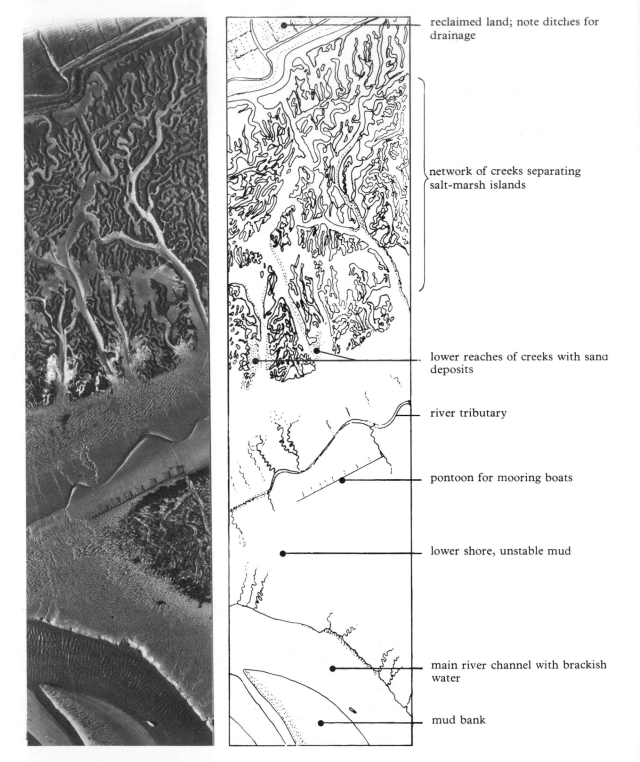

reclaimed land; note ditches for drainage

network of creeks separating salt-marsh islands

lower reaches of creeks with sand deposits

river tributary

pontoon for mooring boats

lower shore, unstable mud

main river channel with brackish water

mud bank

Algal mats and microfauna	Amongst the algal mats covering the creek sides, is a micro-community of protozoans, nematodes, flatworms and microscopic crustaceans like copepods. Taking samples for examination under the microscope will show variation in number, type and density of species through the year.

ANIMALS OF THE SALT-MARSH CREEKS

Gammarus duebeni	(an amphipod, crustacean, up to 15 mm, see also page 49)

- it lives in salt-marsh creek water, burrowing under algae and debris at low tide; it feeds on detritus
- there is a cyclical change in the salinity of the water here; *G. duebeni* is well adapted to regulate the blood concentration within narrow limits: few other organisms can tolerate such extremes

Sphaeroma rugicauda   (an isopod, crustacean, up to 9 mm)

- it lives in the surface sediment and on algae and swims freely at high tide; the larvae are less tolerant of low salinity
- several colour forms exist (polymorphism): red, yellow and grey; the gene frequency depends on the salinity and temperature: yellow has a faster growth rate than grey under cold conditions and larger individuals have a higher chance of survival

Mites

- these are common predators in the drier soil of the levee

Gobius minutus   (sand goby) up to 9 cm in length

- may be found in the water of the creeks at high tide
- it feeds on small crustaceans
- its presence in creeks attracts the attention of terns

Gasterosteus aculeatus   (3-spined stickleback, see also page 49)

- it swims up the creeks at high tide and may become trapped in pools as the tide recedes
- it is well able to cope with osmoregulation
- it feeds on copepods and ostracods

Platichthys flesus   (flounder, see also page 49)

- juveniles live in the wider creeks, moving away with age

Anguilla anguilla   (common eel)

- creeks are used by eels on their migration from freshwater to the sea for feeding and acclimatisation

Birds

Shelduck, as well as feeding on mudflats, move up creeks to feed on *Hydrobia*.

Mallard are omnivores, consuming algal mats and shrimps.

Terns hover over creeks feeding on the fish which move in with the tide.

Gulls scavenge here on materials that wash into the creeks from the salt-marsh.

Redshank is a wader which not only feeds in the creeks but nests on the levee, where it is slightly raised and drier than the surrounding marsh. If there is a very high tide the downy chicks are buoyant and float.

Greenshank and **curlew sandpiper** are the most common wader species to be seen feeding (on crustaceans) in the creek.

Twite overwinters on salt-marshes.

1 *Salicornia europaea* (glasswort)

2 *Spartina* sp. (cord grass)

3 dead and decaying cord grass

4 fragments of seaweeds washed in and caught on salt-marsh plants

5 *Puccinellia maritima* (common salt-marsh grass)

6 mud surface colonised by filamentous algae, stabilising the substrate

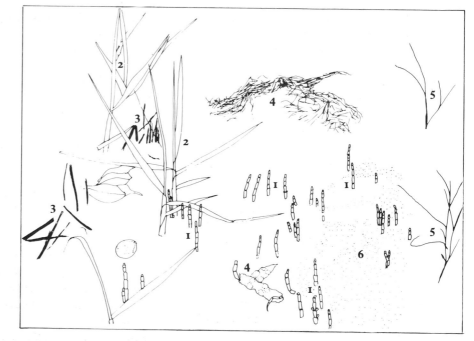

- a high concentration of salt in the sediment; obtaining water is difficult
- the bare sediment is unstable
- for 50% of the day it is covered by the tide, waterlogging the soil
- only the surface of the sediment is aerated, just below is deoxygenated

Spartina species

(cord or rice grass) 1 m in height

- one of the first colonisers of bare mud
- to avoid the anaerobic conditions it grows two types of root: (1) roots in the aerated surface (2) roots in the deeper mud, aerenchyma (tissue with large air spaces) forms two thirds of the tissue; it draws air down from the aerial parts of the stem and this passes out of the roots into the soil to aerate it. Investigation of the root area reveals an orange mud around the roots, an oxidised ferric compound i.e. aerobic respiration occurs.
- the growth of a fine root mass in the top of the mud begins to stabilise the surface
- the deep roots are much larger and anchor the plant against possible wave action
- rhizomes just below the surface are an important asexual method of reproduction; shoots grow off at intervals producing a new plant which allows rapid colonisation
- the biomass of the roots is over two and a half times that of the aerial tissue
- salt glands are present on the leaves to excrete excess salt
- if the concentration of salt is too great the plant sheds leaves with the salt
- a thick cuticle on the leaves, and stomata sunk into deep grooves, slows down transpiration
- it photosynthesises along the C_4 metabolic path unlike temperate land plants; this is more efficient with water, reducing the need by up to 50%
- it is susceptible to shading and is usually found on its own
- it is a high growing plant and so it is affected by drag from water currents and tidal movement; however, this reduces wave action and encourages the deposition of more sediment
- an extensive root system discourages permanent deep burrowing animals
- it is intolerant of intense grazing and is replaced by the common salt-marsh grass in this habitat
- it is affected by the amount of nitrogen in the soil: plants from the lower marsh will be taller than those higher up where there is a greater degree of competition for nitrogen
- by increasing the stability of the mud it can cause extreme stagnation and totally anaerobic conditions; this weakens the plants and may cause 'die-back' i.e. bare patches in the marsh (either in pan form or channels) or stunted growth
- it represents one of the most important producers of detritus in the salt-marsh
- the seeds are dispersed by the tide
- the seeds need low salinity to germinate and do so in spring when freshwater is present

Salicornia europaea

(glasswort) 35 cm in height

- it is one of first colonisers of bare mud, along with *Spartina* although the latter is best suited for very soft mud
- it is an annual plant germinating in April
- it has fleshy succulent stems (no leaves which helps water conservation); succulence allows plenty of water to dilute the high salt content, (comparable with cacti) N.B. no salt glands
- photosynthesis takes place in the stem
- it tolerates grazing
- it is shallow rooted, avoiding the sulphide layer which adversely affects it
- 20% of the root volume is taken up by aerenchyma (air tissue) in the stem bringing air to the roots; this is less than *Spartina* but roots are mainly in the upper aerated area of the substrate
- it cannot tolerate mud in regions of water with strong tidal currents because it is shallow rooted
- sediment accumulates around it

Algae

- *Enteromorpha* and other algae tolerant of variable salinity grow across the mud
- numerous diatoms and blue-green algae live in the surface sediment, secreting mucilage to anchor themselves and reduce water loss
- this algal growth stabilises mud considerably and encourages further deposition to occur; it also enables the glasswort to become established
- mats of algae including *Enteromorpha* and *Ulva* grow under the *Spartina*
- larger algae e.g. *Fucus* may grow in forms called **ecads** amongst the salt-marsh

PLANTS OF THE LOWER SALT-MARSH

Spartina species

This is one of the most important species of the salt-marsh vegetation because it starts the colonisation and the development. It exists in several forms and it is unclear as to whether these are due to genetic or environmental reasons. Competition for nitrogen with other species will limit growth. This may result in stunted *Spartina*.

S. anglica is the most abundant with a hybrid *S. townsendii* a close second. This latter species is an example of a polyploid. It originated from a hybridisation between a European species, *S. stricta* (a diploid chromosome number of 56), and with *S. alterniflora* (a diploid number of 70), an American species, which was introduced to England in about 1870, appearing in Southampton Water and gradually spreading along the coast. The hybrid has a chromosome number of 126, although great variation in this number can occur. Originally the hybrid was sterile and reproduction was limited to asexual propagation by the rhizomes. The appearance of a sexual form has allowed considerable dispersal to occur around the British Isles and across the English Channel. This genetic form grows more vigorously than either of the original parents.

Spartina is very susceptible to pollution from industries found on estuaries and at one time it was believed that this led to the die-back seen on many marshes. *Spartina* is responsible for recycling elements within the ecosystems: iron, zinc, copper, manganese, mercury and, especially, phosphorus. Whilst alive *Spartina* has limited protein value and it is at its highest nutritional stage when virtually decomposed. The litter of decaying leaves and stems collects in autumn and becomes colonised by a bacterial flora which break it down into a rich 'detrital' soup, spilling out with the tide and enriching the estuary. This attracts many animals to come in and feed.

Algal ecads

top: normal *Ascophyllum*
bottom: var *Mackaii* ecad

Ecads are macroalgae deformed by environmental stress not normally encountered, particularly a sheltered and sustained low salinity. They may appear at first to be broken fronds washed up and trapped by the marsh. *Pelvetia* is found in bare patches on the middle marsh. *Ascophyllum* produces such a distinct form it is known as ecad *Mackaii*. Only the air bladders are like the normal form; in common with all ecads it is not attached, rising and falling with the tide. It is a ball of curled fronds which interlocks with others and salt-marsh plants preventing the ecads from being washed away.

Ecads will be replenished by viable fragments of plants washed in by the tide. Zonation of ecads develops where they are abundant (e.g. west coast of Scotland) following the rocky shore zonation pattern.

ADDITIONAL PLANT SPECIES OF THE LOWER SALT-MARSH

Phragmites communis

(common reed) up to 3 m in height
- the tallest European grass
- it replaces *Spartina* as salinity becomes very low at the head of the estuary; a gradual transition occurs as it invades *Spartina* beds
- it tolerates waterlogging by taking air down to the roots via air tissue in the plant

Zostera marina

(eel or sea grass) up to 1 m long, 5–10 mm wide
- it extends to below the lowest water mark
- creeping rhizomes send shoots up and downwards stabilising the shifting mud; this may produce extensive mud banks
- salt glands are present on the leaves
- the leaves create a large biomass that forms detritus on death which encourages a wide diversity of organisms to live upon it
- it is the main diet of Brent geese upon arrival during migration
- it is a water-pollinated flowering plant, not a grass
- this is the species most likely to be encountered, *Z. nana* is a dwarf form, 7–14 cm long and only 0.1 cm wide

See also *Scirpus*, *Puccinellia*, *Enteromorpha*, *Vaucheria*, *Calothrix*, *Pelvetia*, and *Fucus* species.

ANIMALS OF THE LOWER SALT-MARSH

Philaenus spumarius
- a sap-sucking bug found on *Spartina*

Branta bernicla

(Brent goose) 60 cm in height
- it has a black head and chest with a white patch on the side of its neck
- it is a seabird well adapted for marine life, it overwinters on salt-marshes and nests in the Arctic
- migrating south for winter in the British Isles, it starts feeding on *Zostera* (eel grass); after about a month it moves on to *Enteromorpha* and algal mats growing on the mud surface, this corresponds to the time of maximum growth of these plants. In the spring it changes to the higher marsh where it feeds on young salt-marsh grasses e.g. *Puccinellia*.
- salt-marshes are important feeding places for many overwintering birds mainly because the algae grow outside the season of growth of the flowering plants making them productive even in winter
- in the absence of marine food Brent geese are known to move on to agricultural land
- Grey lag geese also overwinter on salt-marsh plants

Anas penelope

(wigeon) 50 cm in height
- a common duck on the lower salt-marsh in winter feeding on eel grass, algae and fescue
- often follows behind the Brent geese as they feed

See also *Hydrobia*, *Corophium*, *Carcinus*, *Shelduck* and waders.
Note: The mud below the *Spartina* beds will correspond to the habitat described in the previous chapter.

SALT PANS

These are small patches of bare mud in the salt-marsh. They often form where developing islands of vegetation merge, isolating bare patches. Some may become colonised but usually they fill with seawater and salt accumulates. In dry weather the salinity becomes intolerably high for plants; rain dilutes it considerably. The glasswort temporarily colonises them but little else can cope with such variable salinity. At high tide animals may become trapped in them, e.g. shrimps, fish, and there are comparisons to be made here with rockpools. When filled with rain-water they are breeding places for insects, notably mosquitoes.

ECOLOGY OF THE SALT-MARSH

General features to look for

- a gradual transition and zonation of species occurs from the strandline to the lower salt-marsh, which is equivalent to the middle of the seashore
- flowering plants dominate the shore with a secondary cover of small algae
- a limited number of plant species are present, they are highly specialised and are called halophytes ('salt lovers')
- it is productive throughout the year, attracting birds in winter
- the animal communities are principally terrestrial with marine species replacing them in the sparser vegetation of the lower shore

The zonation of plants on the salt-marsh is primarily due to differing abilities to cope with salinity and waterlogging of the soil. Zonation of plants may also be due to seedlings being intolerant of salt rather than adults. Most halophytes develop tolerance with age. Animals display a gradual transition of terrestrial species in the upper areas to mud communities lower down, due to the salt content of the plants they graze upon. Several invertebrates are found here which may be associated with one plant species. Where this plant has specialised to the stresses of the environment the animal has become unique. Lower salt-marsh species are detrivores. There is an interesting comparison between other seashore distribution patterns as here it involves the vascular plants (absorbing nutrients through roots) instead of algae which absorb their nutrients through the entire surface and are attached to a hard substrate.

Juncus

Aster(tripolium)

Halimione

Salicornia

Spartina

Zonation of the principal species of the salt-marsh

SUMMARY OF FACTORS AFFECTING SALT-MARSH SPECIES AND ZONATION

1 Salinity varies over the area of the salt-marsh; salt is deposited with the sediment and therefore it is concentrated in the soil making it difficult for vascular plants to obtain water through the roots; the concentration of salt decreases moving up the salt-marsh

2 Waterlogging and oxygen: the tide may cover the plant with seawater but waterlogging of the sediment drives out oxygen and encourages stagnation; vascular plants need to absorb minerals through roots unlike the algae: waterlogging produces reduced inorganic and organic ions as well as toxic chemicals. These are fatal conditions for roots.

3 **Light and submergence**: the seawater which submerges the marsh at high tide is very turbid due to the enormous quantity of detritus; this will seriously restrict light and photosynthesis. It will also restrict gaseous exchange around the leaves. Tidal movement has a dragging effect on the plants and this mechanical force can inflict tissue damage.

4 **Rainfall and freshwater runoff**: drainage is poor on salt-marshes and seepage of water from the land as well as rain will change the salinity. This may affect the osmotic balance of an organism or the germination of seeds. It also allows colonisation by freshwater species.

PLANT ADAPTATIONS TO THE LIMITING FACTORS

- **Tissue with a high solute potential:** to absorb water through the roots a concentration gradient must be maintained so that water flows from the substrate into the plant tissue. Halophytes are the few specialised plants able to absorb and store very high levels of salt in their cells to keep the concentration high enough (i.e. high solute potential, low water potential) for water to pass from the saline soil. This requires expenditure of energy as well as modified metabolism.
- **Salt glands:** these are located on leaves (which tend to have the highest (most negative) solute potential) and consist of a few cells near the surface. They differ among those halophytes which bear them. In most cases ATP is used to pump chloride ions to the cell surface and the difference in the charge pulls sodium ions to the outside. This is an active excretion method.
- **Shedding leaves:** this may be in addition to or instead of salt glands. In the autumn, salt is transported to leaves which are then dropped. Glasswort sheds salt at the end of the season but uses the stem as it does not have leaves. However, leaves can be dropped at any time when the salt content reaches an unacceptable level.
- **Succulence:** this is comparable to cacti and is a way of tolerating high salt content in tissues by compensating with a high water uptake. Succulence also reduces drag, the rounded nature gives a reduced surface area.
- **Air tissue:** with anaerobic conditions in the soil, air is conducted down to the roots through an extensive system of air spaces passing through the stem. *Spartina* contains over 70% air space in the root and diffusion of air into the soil creates aerobic conditions around the root surface. This maintains an oxidising layer in the soil which does not have toxic side effects (see reducing layers and sulphides, page 50).
- **Sclerenchyma:** this needle-like tissue is found in most land plants but halophytes are high in fibres to resist the mechanical stresses of the tide when submerged.
- **Water conservation:** surrounded by salt water the plants conserve the pure water they do obtain. Halophytes have a lower number of stomata per unit area of the leaf than most land plants. Salt-marsh grass can curl leaves and *Spartina* has the stomata in pits to hold moisture.
- **Photosynthesis:** several halophytes have C_4 metabolism. The difference with the more usual C_3 is in the fixing of the CO_2. In C_3 metabolism phosphoglyceric acid (PGA) is the substance produced from the fixation. C_4 plants (mainly tropical species) are those able to use an additional pathway. Here CO_2 reacts with phosphoenolpyruvate (PEP) to give oxaloacetic acid which can then be converted into aspartate or malate. This is within a cycle called the Hatch-Slack cycle. The significance of this to salt-marsh plants is that (a) it requires less CO_2, (b) they can store these substances and hence store CO_2 and (c) it uses less water. For the first of these two it helps the plant to photosynthesise when covered by seawater (reduced gaseous exchange) and less water used helps in conservation of water.

Upper salt-marsh which has been intensively grazed by sheep (note the salt pan)

COLONISATION AND SUCCESSION ON SALT-MARSHES

The zonation on the salt-marsh is a dynamic one involving a change in the communities with time. The speed of replacement of one community over another depends on several factors:

- the rate of supply of sediment
- the degree of shelter afforded to the marsh and
- the topography of the land

Complete succession from mud to a closed salt-marsh community may take 200–500 years.

Algae help to stabilise the surface and allow the initial colonisation by glasswort and cord grass (*Spartina*) although the latter can grow on unstable mud. Glasswort is an annual but the grass is a perennial; *Spartina* has creeping rhizomes which colonise rapidly and the plant may remain on its own for 25 years. During this time it is stabilising the marsh and removing some of the salt. Gradually, other species begin to invade that do not have the pioneering adaptations of the initial colonisers. Competition for nitrogen and light may weaken the *Spartina* and a steady change to a general salt-marsh vegetation occurs. Grazing and freshwater will influence further changes. Creeks which ramify through a salt-marsh may destabilise the marsh as they bring in tidal water. The scouring effect will cause slumping of the banks. The results of erosion may then be secondary colonisation and succession.

Fig. 16 Summary of succession within a salt-marsh (a halosere)

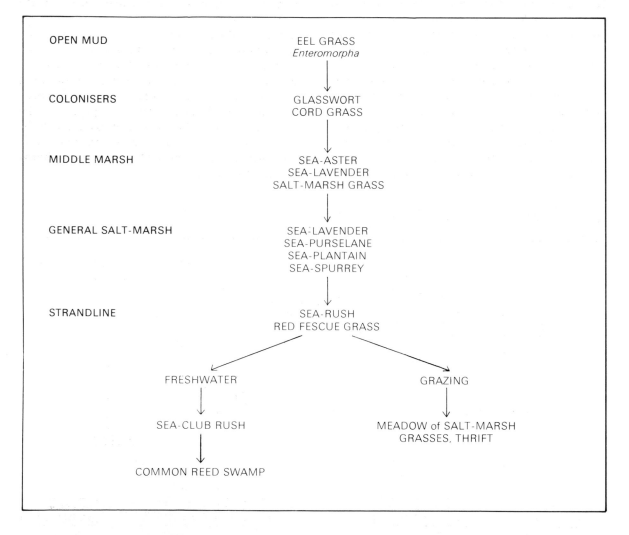

Around the strandline some sand dune and shingle species may occur. For example, lyme grass (*Elymus arenaria*) and sand couch grass (*Agropyron junceiforme*). Dense swathes of shrubby seablite (*Suaeda vera*) sometimes dominate the strandline area if there is shingle present and lower down the marsh a similar species, the annual seablite (*S. maritima*) can grow.

FOOD AND FEEDING RELATIONSHIPS

Diatoms and algae abound, as do bacteria. Salt-marsh plants are productive but by virtue of their adaptations, e.g. thick cuticle, sclerenchyma, they are almost inedible whilst alive. As they decay their nutritious state improves. They are essential to the food web in the production of detritus. Much of this detritus will be transferred to other shores, especially mud and sand. In turn, organic matter arrives from other ecosystems where it becomes trapped amongst the halophytes and then slowly rots. Land plants have been shown to form a third of salt-marsh detritus in some cases.

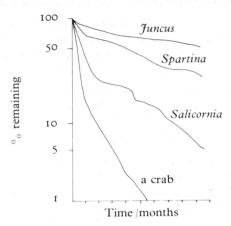

Fig. 17 Decomposition of three salt-marsh plants and an estuarine crab

Decomposition

As the plants decay their calorific value to animals actually rises partly due to the growth of bacteria and fungi on the material. At the start there is a sudden loss in weight as soluble substances wash out. *Spartina* is high in lignin, which gives support and protects it from mechanical damage. Lignin takes almost three times as long to decay as cellulose. As well as the microflora breaking up the leaf and stem litter, there is considerable physical breakdown from tidal action and temperature; smaller particles are more quickly decomposed by bacteria.

The consumers

Detritus is colonised and consumed by ciliate and flagellate protozoans. They feed mainly on the saprophytic bacteria. As decay proceeds consumption by crustaceans and molluscs increases the decomposition still further. This is because as they void the detritus as faeces it increases the nitrogen content, encouraging bacterial growth. (See also faecal soup page 54.) The upper marsh may be used for grazing by sheep and cattle. Intense grazing produces a very fine turf with a poor variety of animals (see photograph on page 71).

Fig. 18 Simplified food web of a salt-marsh

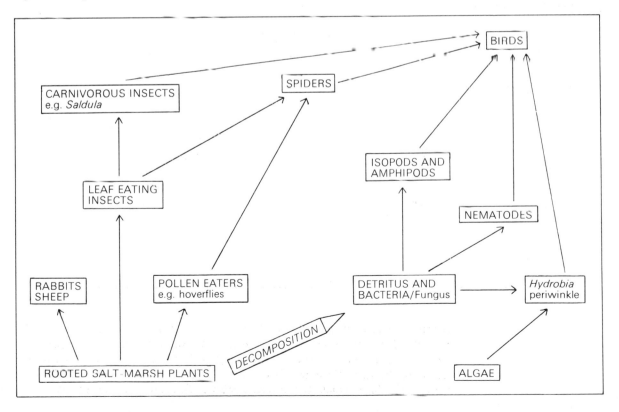

Question 1

The table shows the solute potentials of cell sap of various salt-marsh plants and the amount of chloride ion as a percentage of that solute potential. (Reprinted with permission from Chapman, 1976, Pergamon Books Ltd.)

Species	Solute potential /atm.	Cl⁻ % of sap *solute potential*
Spear-leaved orache (*Atriplex hastata*)	−31.6	42
Seablite (*Suaeda* sp.)	−35.2	43
Sea rush (*Juncus* sp.)	−27.8	56
Sea club-rush (*Scirpus maritimus*)	−14.7	71
Glasswort (*Salicornia* sp.)	−44.3	71
Cord grass (*Spartina* sp.)	−39.7	91

a Discuss the possibility of relating sap solute potential with the position of the plant on the salt-marsh.

b What is the significance of chloride ions as a percentage of the sap solute potential in your answer to part **a**?

Question 2

The tabulated data are the percentage germination of salt-marsh plants after a 28 day period in different salinities. (From Chapman, 1976)

	Tap water			Seawater		
	alone	+1% NaCl	+2% NaCl	alone	+5% NaCl	+10% Nacl
Spartina townsendii	80	21	15	3	0	0
Phragmites communis	4	36	16	0	0	0
Aster tripolium	45	25	10	0	0	0
Salicornia sp.	93	45	36	38	36	12
Suaeda sp.	4	0	4	0	0	0
Juncus maritimus	50	18	5	0	0	0
Halimione portulacoides	83	50	8	0	0	0

a Discuss the data with regard to colonisation and succession of the salt-marsh species.

b What other factors should be taken into account when considering the seed germination of these plants?

c Under optimum conditions *Spartina* has the ability to germinate rapidly, compared with most other salt-marsh plants. How could this benefit its pioneering ability in mud?

PROJECTS ON THE SALT-MARSH

A belt transect is the best form of transect to use over a narrow band of salt-marsh so that a map of distribution can be constructed. The small number of species present adds to the clarity of the result.

One of the most important aspects of the salt-marsh is the decay of vegetation providing detritus for consumption by various organisms. To compare the rate of decay of different plant species is a worthwhile exercise. This can be studied by regular weighing of samples of the dead plants at weekly intervals which are tied up in small muslin bags. This could be compared under different conditions such as increased or decreased temperature.

A 'hay' infusion made with *Spartina* in seawater can be used to study the colonisation and succession of micro-organisms on the decaying leaves.

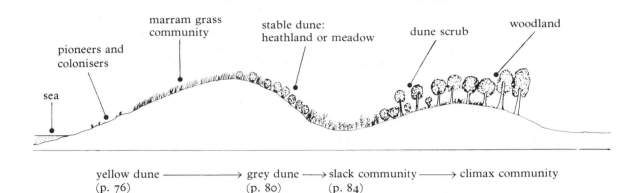

yellow dune ——————→ grey dune ——→ slack community ——————→ climax community
(p. 76)   (p. 80)   (p. 84)

Fig. 19 A profile across a sand dune habitat

SUBSTRATE

- the sand deposited on the beach forming the dunes may be eroded rock e.g. silica, or tiny fragments of shell
- the type of sand strongly influences the eventual development of sand dune communities

SAND DUNE FORMATION

- sand is carried inshore by currents and deposited at high tide
- the water drains away from the beach at low tide; drying continues in the wind and sun
- the dry sand is the source of material for the formation of the dunes; the amount is one of the factors in limiting the height and general size of the dune system
- wind is crucial in the development; as wind blows the dry sand along the beach, any object projecting upwards will be struck by the particles, which collect on the leeward side
- inanimate objects cease to collect sand once they are covered
- plants that can survive in this very harsh environment, e.g. sand couch, grow by rhizomes, which spread out, under the sand surface
- plants become covered by sand and this stimulates them to grow above it; more sand hits the plant and collects, and so on, gradually increasing the height of the hillock; the final height depends on the amount of wind blown sand

THE COMMUNITIES

- the earliest colonisers may be termed pioneers and they help in developing embryo dunes e.g. saltwort
- gradually they are replaced by marram grass: which increases the extent and stability of the dunes; with virtually no soil and only yellow sand visible it is called a **yellow dune**
- with increased stability, more species colonise the dune, e.g. heather; with increased organic matter the dune soil becomes much darker – a **grey dune**
- areas near the water table or depressions in the dune become damp, even marshy – **dune slacks**
- after several hundred years scrubland may develop into woodland – the **climax community**

PROBLEMS AND FEATURES OF SAND DUNES

- water content is so low the plants are called **xerophytes** and have adaptations to conserve water e.g. slow transpiration, extensive root systems to find water
- wind and salt increase the problem of water
- soils are very fragile; trampling and burrowing by rabbits can break through the soil releasing fresh wind-blown sand to create **blow-outs**; they can cause massive erosion
- conditions are not so extreme as in a salt-marsh and a very diverse range of species may be present

POINTS OF SPECIAL INTEREST

- to study colonisation and succession
- adaptations of xerophytes in water conservation

1 *Ammophila arenaria* (marram grass)

2 *Eryngium maritimum* (sea-holly)

3 *Euphorbia paralias* (sea-spurge)

4 *Festuca rubra* (red fescue)

5 *Carex arenaria* (sand sedge)

6 *Hypochaeris radicata* (cat's ear)

7 *Matthiola incana* (sea-stock)

8 *Helix aspersa* (common garden snail)

PROBLEMS
- the dunes are very unstable, with wind-blown sand; they may be mobile
- very low water content
- salt is laid down with the sand but gradually removed by rainwater
- soil and humus are non-existent, limited availability of mineral ions
- extremes of temperature
- desiccating wind increases water loss

Ammophila arenaria

(marram grass) 1 m in height
- it dominates the yellow dune
- it is an upright grass which colonises by an extensive rhizome system
- along the rhizome leaves grow up to the surface whilst adventitious roots radiate out to collect water
- if the leaves are covered by sand, buds at the bases produce shoots which break through to the surface and grow another tuft of leaves
- tracing back along the shoot the position of the last growth can be found (the node); the spaces between growth points is the internode. The length of internode varies with the depth of sand cover. In a bad winter the deposition of sand could be in metres and this can be measured on the shoot internode.
- the rhizome system penetrates deep into the dune which it has helped to create and with the lateral adventitious roots is able to obtain water
- it is intolerant of salt in the sand and does not colonise until rainwater has washed most salt away
- transpiration is slowed by a thick shiny cuticle on the upper epidermis
- stomata on the lower epidermis are sunk into pits and surrounded by spines to reduce water loss; this is furthered by the presence of hinge cells that curl the leaf according to the level of external humidity; in sunshine the leaf is tightly curled whilst if it is raining the leaf is flattened
- as marram dominates it reduces wind action over the dune, which, in turn, reduces mobile sand and increases stability
- with a change in the microclimate the open community of marram is colonised by other plants
- in the absence of a new sand covering, the tussock of marram gradually rots, contributing organic matter to the soil

Eryngium maritimum (sea-holly)
- a low-growing perennial which is a member of the carrot family; a blue umbel flower
- it is a halophytic plant able to tolerate salty sand
- with a tolerance for salt it can colonise sand before marram grass
- it has a fleshy tap root and is able to store water in it
- it produces an extensive root system up to 2 m in length
- the leaves are leathery with a thick cuticle to reduce water loss; the grey-green bloom is due to a wax coating
- the roots produce a very low osmotic potential to absorb water from the sand
- like marram it is able to grow out of a sand covering; the shoot lengthens and the internodes can be measured for the depth of sand
- the flowers are especially attractive to insects
- tides disperse the buoyant seeds

Euphorbia paralias (sea-spurge)
- it has a red stem and oval, succulent leaves; the leaves have a leathery surface and thick cuticle; in very dry conditions the leaves fold together
- succulence is a way of overcoming a high salt content in the tissues which is necessary in maintaining a low osmotic potential
- it has the ability to grow out of a sand covering; as sand covers the leaves so they die off leaving a scar; the stem branches after major coverings and produces the clumps visible in the picture on page 76
- like other members of the spurge family the plant has a white, milky sap

Carex arenaria (sand sedge)
- invariably the individual plants are found arranged in lines; all are shoots from the same rhizome running about 15 cm under the surface; a dense mat of sedge stabilises the sand
- it is intolerant of salt and a deep sand covering and is normally found where the dunes are more stable

Helix aspersa (common garden snail)
- its presence is a sign of calcium (shell sand)

Matthiola incana (sea-stock)
- a rarity, found on dunes

ADDITIONAL SPECIES OF THE YELLOW DUNE

PLANT PIONEER SPECIES

Cakile maritima

(sea-rocket)
- a member of the cabbage family; the fruits are dispersed by the tide and it may form a dominant covering on the shore
- it obtains much of its nutrients from decayed remains of items washed up on the strandline
- it is a halophyte, but it cannot tolerate submersion in seawater
- the succulent leaves help tolerate a high internal salt content which produces an exceptionally high solute potential for absorbing water; it has extremely long roots

Salsola kali

(prickly saltwort)
- a low-growing, prostrate halophyte living below the dunes
- the succulent leaves and stem store water
- it has a huge root system, both horizontal and vertical, which extends for several metres
- a very high solute potential is maintained
- it does get covered by sand through which it can grow, producing embryonic dunes below the main marram ones

Agropyron junceiforme

(sand couch grass) 20–40 cm in height, it can grow taller
- it is tolerant of salt and is therefore the first grass to be found on the beach and is an important species since it initiates the building of the dunes
- a rhizome runs horizontally sending up shoots above the sand but the extent of vertical growth is limited to 40–50 cm; hence it cannot compete with marram grass in cases of greater amounts of wind blown sand; the leaves are not very long and tend to droop over, making them poor collectors of sand; it has no leaf ligule like marram
- it is prone to attack by cigar gall flies: swelling at the leaf base results

Elymus arenarius

(lyme grass) 1–1.5 m tall
- often found with marram and couch grass as a dune builder
- it is intolerant of high temperatures and hence is limited to northern Europe; in Iceland it is the dominant dune plant
- the leaves can roll like marram in dry weather to enclose the stomata, reducing water loss
- unlike marram the leaves are lost in autumn; this makes the dune less stable and so lyme grass is usually found amongst the marram
- it is susceptible to rust and smut fungi, these can be seen as sooty deposit on the stem and leaves

Calystegia soldanella

(sea-convolvulus)
- a prostrate perennial which grows amongst the dune grasses producing trumpet flowers (white with pink stripes)
- it has kidney-shaped, succulent leaves for water storage
- creeping rhizomes spread the plant vegetatively and it is a favourite food of rabbits, which can severely limit its distribution
- it is halophytic with a high salt content to maintain a very low osmotic potential

See also *Atriplex* (orache, page 59) and *Honkenya* (page 95).

A community on a yellow dune from a silica sand

1 *Ammophila arenaria (marram grass)*

2 *Hypochaeris radicata* (cat's ear)

3 *Jasione montana* (sheep's bit)

4 *Festuca rubra* (red fescue)

5 rabbit droppings

6 shell of the banded snail which has been eaten by other snails

Although at this stage in succession there are not many clear differences between the silica dune and those with a degree of shell sand, sea-holly and sea-spurge are notably absent. Silica dunes are very low in nutrients and rely on wind-borne organic matter e.g. dry fragments of seaweed.

Hypochoeris radicata

(common cat's ear)

- a rosette plant; the leaves are pressed out flat on to the surface of the sand, any water transpired from the lower epidermis will condense back into the sand
- beneath the rosette is a long tap root which stores water; lateral roots obtain the water
- it is able to tolerate a slight rise in the sand cover; the tap root can keep the leaves supported until the plant has grown through the sand
- yellow flowers are borne on elongated stems which can grow through the marram tussock for pollination by insects

Jasione montana

(sheep's bit)

- a biennial flower which grows in closely growing units to reduce water loss; it has a long root system

ANIMALS OF THE YELLOW DUNES

Invertebrates

Insects and snails are the most abundant invertebrates on dunes although overall there is a paucity due to the limited and coarse vegetation. Harvestmen spiders feed on the visiting insects. The number of snails varies with the degree of calcium.

Vertebrates

Rabbits are abundant on dunes, possibly because of the easy burrowing. Their droppings increase the soil humus content as far down the shore as the embryo dunes. They dig down to feed on the rhizomes. Gulls nesting on the dunes improve the soil nitrogen content.

GREY DUNE COMMUNITY
with shell sand present (alkaline)

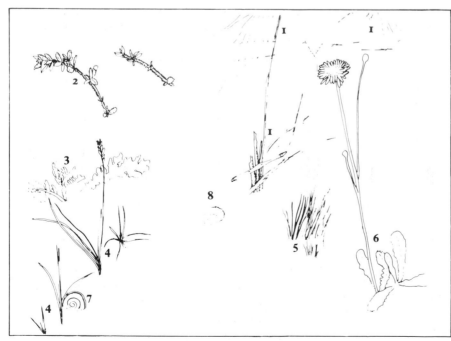

1 dead and dying marram grass

2 *Cerastium* sp. (mouse-ear chickweed)

3 *Senecio jacobaea* (ragwort)

4 *Carex arenaria* (sand sedge)

5 *Festuca rubra* (red fescue)

6 *Hypochoeris radicata* (cat's ear)

7 *Cepaea nemoralis* (banded snail)

8 *Helix aspersa* (common garden snail)

- very shallow and fragile soil
- very low water content
- more sheltered and stable than the yellow dune with little or no wind-blown sand
- possible shading of smaller plants by marram, both dead and alive
- a wide range of species can live here especially if shell sand is present; most will be occasional colonisers and specific to an area; some of the commoner species are given here

---

Ammophila arenaria (marram grass)

- due to the lack of wind-blown sand the marram begins to fail and tussocks break up to produce a considerable quantity of leaf litter
- the marram provides shelter so that other plant species now begin to grow beneath it
- a break in the thin soil crust will release sand which would rejuvenate the marram: a blow out; this would start erosion of the dune and the cycle of dune formation would begin again

Carex arenaria (sand sedge)

- this sedge colonises after the marram grass and is one of the most important plants of the dune for stabilising the ground
- colonisation is essentially by the rhizome; growth can be up to 4 m per year
- the rhizome grows approximately 15 cm below the sand surface and runs in relatively straight lines, sending up tufts of leaves at the nodes
- these tufts grow off the triangular stem in groups of three to give a 'star-like' appearance from above
- the tufts reduce wind action on the soil surface and the 'weave' of rhizomes, as they criss-cross the dunes, both help in increasing stability
- the asexually produced tufts of leaves develop a flower; they can be seen growing in straight lines, showing where the rhizome is buried beneath
- this rapid colonisation will produce clonal groupings e.g. the individuals in the photo (page 82) will, most likely, be genetically identical

Cerastium species (mouse ear chickweed)

- it is an annual plant whose seeds germinate in the autumn when water is plentiful; this produces an abundance of seedlings in the spring
- to survive the desiccation it dies early in summer surviving in seed form

Hypochoeris radicata (common cat's ear)

- a widespread plant of most dunes, see page 79

Senecio jacobaea (ragwort)

- a common biennial of grassland
- after germination the large leaves form a loose rosette on the sand in the autumn and winter when the dunes are at their wettest
- in the second year of growth an extensive root system develops which is a necessary adaptation to survive the summer months
- a tall yellow flower develops in the second year; dead flower heads remain until the following year and are conspicuous
- the plant cells contain cyanide and few organisms eat the leaves. The yellow and black larva of the cinnabar moth does eat it; the adult colour is red and black and in both stages the colour warns of being distasteful to possible predators.

Festuca species (fescue grass)

- these fine-leaved grasses (reduced surface area for conserving water) further increase stability of the dunes
- red fescue is a pioneer grass as it can grow in nutrient-poor soils; other fescue species colonise when the soil quality improves

ADDITIONAL PLANT SPECIES

Centaurium littorale (seaside centaury)

- it has a pink flower and is related to the gentians
- its niche lies along a gradient of wet–dry sand
- it is capable of being a pioneer species on bare, saline sand
- it is affected by the water table and if this changes then so does the population density i.e. if the seeds are saturated then germination is delayed
- if the seedlings are submerged in water they become stunted

Other species commonly encountered are the tall, blue bugloss, yellow clustered stonecrop, ladies bedstraw, thyme and yarrow. Mosses form dense patches; they are important stabilisers.

GREY DUNE COMMUNITY
without shell sand (acidic)

1 dead and dying marram grass

2 *Calluna vulgaris* (ling) mature plants

3 young ling plant colonising

4 lichens growing on the sand surface

5 mosses growing on the sand surface

6 *Carex arenaria* (sand sedge)

7 rabbit droppings

PROBLEMS and FEATURES
- very shallow and fragile soil
- very low water content
- more sheltered and stable than yellow dune with little wind-blown sand
- possible shading of smaller plants by marram, both dead and alive
- any shells incorporated into the dunes are whole and calcium is very low; any minerals are leached out by rainwater: soil is poor in bases; the result is an acid soil, pH 3.5–5: this is a specialised niche for organisms and is typically heathland

Calluna vulgaris (the ling)
- a bush heather which produces large numbers of tiny seeds (wind dispersed), enabling quick colonisation
- germination requires a wet soil and the seeds usually start to develop in autumn; rapid growth ensures a suitable overwintering plant, growth slows in summer months
- seeds need light for germination and young plants develop in open places on the dune; the seeds remain viable for many years and only when the shading effect of marram declines will the ling begin to grow
- after 20–30 years the bush begins to collapse exposing the centre containing deep leaf litter; young birch trees may become established here
- conservation of water is important; the leaves have a very reduced surface area and are compacted together; stomata are opened and closed according to the turgidity of the plant, rather than set in pits like other heathers, giving greater control
- the roots have an association with a fungus called *Phoma*; this assists ling with its mineral needs (e.g. nitrogen) by localised decomposition
- as the ling ages its woody stem become colonised by lichens

Lichens
- lichens make up an important part of a heather community; up to 30 species may be present
- they are especially common when rabbits are present
- lichens can completely cover the surface of the sand making an important contribution to sand stabilisation
- the fungal component is able to absorb and hold water for long periods
- dozens of species grow on fixed dunes and they show a distinct zonation
- as the ling ages they gradually colonise the woody stems

Mosses
- the number of mosses growing on the sand surface increases with stability
- they are not tolerant of shading
- grazing by rabbits may cause a decline in mosses
- by growing in very tight cushions, excessive water loss is reduced

Carex arenaria (sand sedge, see page 81)
- found on most dune systems and not associated with any one plant community

ADDITIONAL PLANT SPECIES ON ACIDIC GREY DUNES

Erica cineraria (bell heather)
- it is a well adapted xerophyte with needle shaped leaves; the stomata are set in pits and covered by spines

Pteridium aquilinum (bracken)
- upon invading a heath it may shade out other species, becoming dominant with ling

Ulex species (gorse)
- this becomes established after the heathers
- when established its persistent growth will shade out other plants
- the stems and leaves are reduced to spines to conserve water; both are photosynthetic
- root nodules improve nitrogen uptake

ANIMAL SPECIES ON ACIDIC GREY DUNES

Lochmaea suturalis (heather beetle)
- it feeds on ling and may lead to defoliation
- a small rounded brown beetle; it pupates in the raw humus below the ling

Macrothylacia rubi (fox moth)
- the larva feeds on the heathers until autumn and then hibernates; in spring it resumes feeding, then pupates; the moth flies during the day and night

DUNE SLACK COMMUNITY

with shell sand present (alkaline)

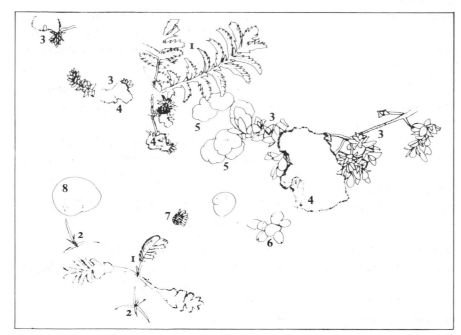

1 *Potentilla anserina* (silverweed)

2 *Carex* spp. (sedges)

3 *Salix repens* (creeping willow)

4 willow in flower

5 *Hydrocotyle vulgaris* (marsh pennywort)

6 *Lotus corniculatus* (bird's-foot trefoil)

7 *Bellis perennis* (daisy)

8 *Helix aspersa* (common garden snail)

WET ALKALINE SLACKS

PROBLEMS and FEATURES
- these are the flat 'lows' behind the dune system
- closeness to the water table and condensation at night produce a damp soil
- during winter the water table rises giving temporary flooding
- there is stable soil but it is low in nitrogen and phosphorus as earlier leaching will have removed them

---

Salix repens (creeping willow)

- the creeping stems produce a prostrate form over the surface
- it will dominate the slack and can grow into dense bushes
- an extensive root system (up to 10 m total length) assists in obtaining nutrients from the poor soil
- the prostrate stems will also take root
- it recovers well from erosion or minor sand coverings and therefore colonises the slacks early on in the succession
- any wind-blown sand reaching the slack will accumulate around the willow, forming small hummocks; this results in a drier habitat and other plants can move in to colonise
- it cannot survive a permanently waterlogged soil and its distribution is therefore limited
- dry areas allow tall vegetation whilst the wetter it becomes the more prostrate it grows
- a dense leaf litter forms beneath; much humus is generated by the willow
- the fluffy patches are the seeds

Potentilla anserina (silverweed)

- a fine mat of hairs gives a shiny, white surface to the leaf
- its runners creep over the surface of the soil entangling with the willow
- it is typical of damp grassy places and its presence here reflects the occasional flooding that must occur

Hydrocotyle vulgaris (marsh pennywort)

- it has a distinct circular leaf with the petiole arising from the centre
- typical of damp places it is a prostrate creeping perennial; a sign here of occasional flooding

Agrostis stolonifera (creeping bent grass)

- unlike the grasses already seen it does not have a rhizome, instead it possesses stolons, which penetrate through the prolific willow roots

Carex species (sedges)

- in the wet soil several species can be found below the willow; their star-like appearance of three leaves is a characteristic due to the triangular stem
- rhizomes disperse underground, shooting upwards and develop into new plants
- *C. flacca* (glaucous sedge) favours calcareous damp grassland and may be dwarfed in the undergrowth
- *C. nigra* (common sedge) is common on most damp grassland

Lotus corniculatus (birdsfoot trefoil)

- the yellow flower is usually tinged with red
- a creeping, prostrate perennial plant with an extensive root system for obtaining nutrients
- it is not unique to dunes but widespread in grasslands generally

Bellis perennis (common daisy)

- a common species on damp dune grassland
- its flattened, rosette leaves tolerate grazing and conserve water

Cepaea nemoralis (brown lipped snail)

- the commonest snail on dunes, most abundant in the damper regions
- it is an example of genetic polymorphism, where several colour forms are present: yellow, pink, brown and striped

ADDITIONAL SPECIES OF DUNE SLACKS

Juncus acutus (the spike rush)

- it grows in dense stands where waterlogging occurs; aerenchyma takes air down to the roots
- it is tolerant of salt

Plantago coronopus (bucksthorn plantain)

- a flat rosette form which is common at the start of slacks; very tolerant of grazing
- it is tolerant of slight salinity
- it cannot compete with creeping willow which shades it out

FLOODED DUNE SLACK COMMUNITY
without shell sand (acidic)

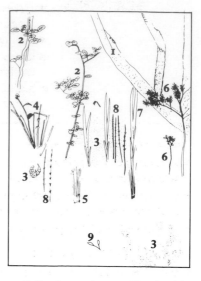

1 *Salix cinerea* (grey willow) with lichens on bark

2 *Alnus glutinosa* (alder)

3 *Sphagnum* spp. (bog mosses)

4 Ferns

5 *Molinia caerulea* (purple moor grass)

6 *Myrica gale* (bog myrtle)

7 *Iris pseudacorus* (yellow iris)

8 *Equisetum fluviatile* (water horsetail), colonises the marshy areas by rhizomes; at the top a fertile cone is produced

9 *Ranunculus flammula* (lesser spearwort)

WET, FLOODED ACIDIC SLACKS

PROBLEMS and FEATURES
- these are the flat 'lows' behind the dune system
- closeness to the water table and flooding links the low ground to give a continuous marsh or bog; they are therefore waterlogged
- during winter the water table rises giving temporary flooding
- it has a stable soil but is very low in nitrogen and phosphorus as earlier leaching will have removed them
- high acidity will reduce decomposition and limit the establishment of many plants and animals

Salix cinerea (grey willow)
- several types of willow will grow, all of which attain a 5–10 m height
- it restricts the light reaching the ground, and therefore the presence of many flowers
- it is tolerant of the permanent waterlogging

Alnus glutinosa (the alder)
- the root nodules fix nitrogen which may be used by other plants in the community
- their presence in a slack depends on the intensity of rabbit grazing; in this habitat it is too wet for rabbits whilst in drier areas alder may survive due to the disappearance of rabbits because of myxomatosis
- the seeds float (water dispersal) and need light to germinate; hence found on the edge of the slack where there is less shade

Sphagnum species (bog mosses)
- a characteristic species of acid bogs
- it holds water like a sponge and so even during dry summers the moss retains water, supplying other species which live in it
- a succession of bog mosses develop, the first in standing water followed by ones able to live above it in progressively drier conditions; this creates a hummock which in turn will be colonised by heathers and grasses; when almost a metre high it may collapse and the succession starts again
- it is an important species, therefore, in the establishment and development of the slack
- after death the acidic and waterlogged (lack of oxygen) conditions will prevent decomposition; it accumulates to form peat

Ferns
- ferns cope well under the willow canopy since they are shade tolerant
- water is essential for their reproduction and they have no adaptations to cope with water loss
- the largest European fern, *Osmunda regalis*, the royal fern, is locally abundant in some dune slacks

Molinia caerulea (purple moor-grass)
- it grows well on wet peaty soils
- it usually requires an inflow of freshwater bringing nutrients

Myrica gale (bog myrtle)
- it has a distinct sweet smell when rubbed between fingers; it grows as a small bush (sparse under the willow canopy)
- it is a key species in the bog where mineral ions are rare; root nodules release nitrates

Iris pseudacorus (yellow iris)
- a common marsh plant found in standing water

ADDITIONAL SPECIES ON ACIDIC WET SLACKS

Erica tetralix (cross-leaved heather)
- the only heather to tolerate waterlogged soil
- it normally grows in a rounded bush but when shaded it becomes more sparse

Drosera rotundifolia (common sundew)
- an insectivorous annual plant; it is adapted to catch and digest insects to obtain basic mineral ions (nitrates, phosphates, etc.) which cannot be obtained from the soil

Ranunculus flammula (lesser spearwort)
- creeping runners establish it in the peat, the leaves are seen floating on standing water

Phragmites communis (common reed)
- it may develop large stands, see page 68.
- *Juncus* species grow throughout the slacks (page 85).

See also pennywort, creeping willow and sedges.

ANIMAL SPECIES

Mosquitoes breed in the stagnant pools and these are consumed by the damselflies and dragonflies, which are a common sight on dune slacks. A number of amphibians breed here and the rare natterjack toad is typical of the conditions provided by the habitat in both acid and alkali pools.

COLONISATION AND SUCCESSION OF SAND DUNE COMMUNITIES

General trends/to look for:

- there is a zonation of vegetation inland from the sea
- this zonation is not static but is gradually changing as one community replaces another

FEATURES OF SUCCESSION

The pioneer species can tolerate a wide range of environmental stresses. Sea rocket and prickly kale will colonise bare sand near the strandline, obtaining much of their mineral ions from organic matter washed up on the beach. Although tolerant of salt they cannot cope with being buried too deep by the unstable, wind-blown sand. But sand couch can and soon develops embryonic dunes as the sand collects around it. Marram colonises when the salt has leached away, and shades out the other grasses. It thrives on wind-blown sand. Its rhizomes can grow to amazing depths and its ability to conserve water soon makes it the dominant species above the high tide mark of sandy shores. The dune continues to grow, some to 30 m in height, but as it does so it changes the wind profile and, depending on the degree of wind and sand, the growth slows. The increased stability spells its death: the lack of wind-blown sand eventually causes the break up of the marram tussocks, although rhizomes continue growing underground from stored food.

As stability increases, so does soil quality. To start with it was no more than the inorganic sand but, with time, debris from the plants and rabbit droppings help to develop a shallow soil. This encourages plants not so well adapted to the harshness of early colonisation and the species diversity increases. Where the dune slacks are near the water table, the water content increases and a different community forms.

If shell sand is present the dunes remain alkaline, encouraging downland plants and animals. On sheltered coasts the sand will be inert silica and the shells are washed up intact. As the dunes build so the shells remain at the original level with all the calcium locked inside. The result is that the dune becomes acidic and very poor in minerals. This typically forms a heathland community. Each community in this succession is called a **sere** and a transect across the dune will reveal several distinct seres until one becomes stable and remains: the **climax community**.

Fig. 20 Summary of succession of sand dune communities

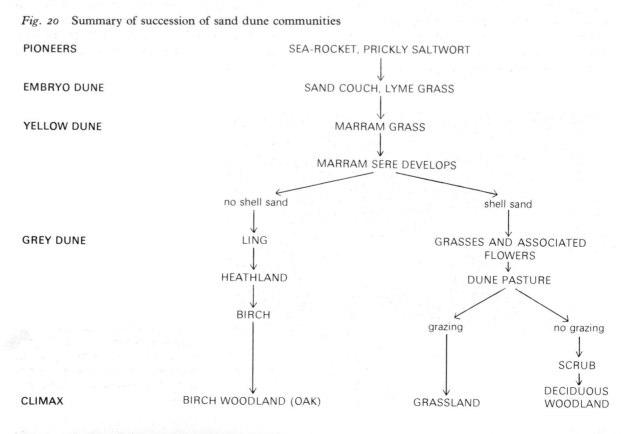

ECOLOGICAL SUCCESSION

Aspects to look for:

- the height and differentiation of the communities increase with age
- development of the soil takes place with time, including an increase in depth, humus content, water content and formation of soil horizons (layering, seen in a soil profile)
- productivity increases with the development of the soil and communities
- the communities begin to affect the microclimate around them as succession progresses e.g. the wind action, temperature
- the diversity of species changes from a few at the start to many later when the environmental harshness has lessened and fewer specialised adaptations are necessary for survival
- there is a gradual replacement of one community by another but the speed slows with age e.g. marram may remain dominant for 30 years, ling 50 years and birch 100's of years
- the stability of the community increases with age; marram and the soil at the start is unstable and easily breaks down with erosion; as time goes on blow-outs become less likely as the soil increases in depth

BLOW-OUTS AND CONSERVATION

The soil is like a thin skin over the surface of the sand; once broken, erosion starts and the hole enlarges revealing more and more sand. Eventually the blow-out, as it becomes known, can be 40 m across, decimating a large area of dune. As the rhizomes and roots are exposed they soon die releasing their grip on the sand and increasing the destabilisation. The release of so much sand stimulates the regrowth of marram grass and the process of succession starts again.

For centuries man has understood the value of marram in this respect and it has long been law in the Hebrides in Scotland, where crofters owe their living to the machair dunes, to replant a tussock of marram when a break in the surface was seen. Today, many dunes have replanting programmes and people are asked to walk on duck-board paths to reduce the erosion.

MACHAIR VEGETATION AND SOIL

On the north and west coast of Scotland the extreme wave action smashes shells to produce sand dunes almost entirely of shell sand. The result is a dune system which develops as before but results in a unique pasture land. The calcium carbonate levels reach 90% although other minerals, e.g. nitrates, are lacking. Windy conditions may spread the dunes inland, covering blanket bogs and moorland, and climbing up the sides of headlands. For many years it has been used by crofters for grazing their cattle and sheep. Minor cultivation in the growth of barley and rye has taken place

Grazing has not been intense and use of pesticides is unusual, resulting in a wealth of plants and animals. Dominated by the yellow ladies' bedstraw and red wild thyme, it is one of the last refuges of the corn marigold (killed off elsewhere by pesticides). Slacks behind the dunes will also be highly alkaline. With the high rainfall machair lochs develop which are very rich in fauna

A blow out on a grey dune heath, note the exposed roots of the ling and the shallow soil; slumping of the edges occur as the roots die; marram grass recolonises due to the exposed sand

STUDYING SAND DUNES

The colonisation and succession of sand dune communities is the main point of study. This ecological concept is especially worth considering here as the number of species is low to begin with and the changes that occur are usually very clear.

- use a transect with sample points at intervals of 30 m; if possible construct a profile of the transect
- at each point record the % cover of vegetation by random quadrats
- for invertebrates (i) using a sweep net at each sample point will collect many organisms from the vegetation (ii) set pitfalls traps (glass jam jars) on the sample points across the dunes and empty them at night and morning; this sample of the active animals and their numbers can be related to time of day, weather, vegetation, etc.
- collect soil samples at the different points and later test for pH, organic matter and water content; it is also worth measuring the depth of stable soil (thickness of soil crust at the surface)
- use a Tullgren funnel to extract soil organisms from the samples and compare them: this shows the micro-succession of organisms as the soil develops
- additional data that should be collected is (i) wind speed and (ii) temperature at different heights above the sand
- transpiration is worth studying in the field by using bubble potometers; choose plants from the yellow and grey dune as well as the slacks and compare the rates of water uptake and relate them to leaf surface area; try measuring the rate in different regions e.g. in dune hollows and crests
- plot histograms of the change in species across the dunes

Question 1

The following data was collected from an alkaline, stable sand dune area in July. The results are the total numbers of specimens collected from 18 pitfall traps placed in a line, 2 m apart.

	DAY 1		DAY 2		DAY 3		DAY 4		DAY 5	
Time when pitfalls emptied	0800	2000	0800	2000	0800	2000	0800	2000	0800	2000
No. of cockchafers	48	0	36	1	13	4	28	2	39	3
No. of ground beetles	11	2	14	3	23	1	6	3	18	2
No. of snail beetle	0	0	0	0	5	2	0	1	0	0
No. of wolf spiders	0	28	0	15	0	1	1	11	2	7
No. of ticks	0	1	2	1	1	3	0	1	0	2
No. of millipedes	18	0	23	3	11	8	17	2	14	5
No. of springtails	104	132	81	74	49	66	40	22	11	4
Climate (R = rain, D = dry, H = humid)	D	D	D	DH	R	DH	DH	D	D	D

a Plot a graph of the cockchafer, ground beetles, snail beetle and wolf spider data.

b Which species show a diurnal rhythm? Discuss their activity.

c The snail beetle feeds exclusively on snails. How does this relate to the data given above?

d Ticks do not seem to show any pattern in their activity. Suggest what stimuli could govern their movements.

e Springtails do not move far from their habitat. What is the basic trend shown by the data? Can you suggest reasons for this?

INTRODUCTION

Shingle beaches are the poorest of all maritime habitats. Its instability and rapid drainage requires well adapted plants to colonise it. There are few plant species that are able to survive here and the number of species present is very low. Unlike, say, dunes there is not one characteristic species colonising the shingle.

THE SUBSTRATE

- it is typically composed of rounded pebbles with a gradation of size down or along the shore
- the size will influence which species are able to colonise and develop e.g. the extensive shingle beach at Dungeness in England has small shingle ridges; the troughs, although more sheltered, remain uncolonised whilst the tops have sea kale due to the finer stones that are present
- there may be overlap with sand dunes as material can be laid down with the pebbles or be blown here from nearby dunes; north Norfolk in England has many dune systems overlying shingle beaches; the presence of any silt and sand will increase the chance of plant invasion

SHINGLE BEACH FORMATION

- three main features affect the formation:
  1 the strength and direction of wave action
  2 the size and quantity of pebbles
  3 the range of tidal movement
- four types of shingle beach can be recognised:
  1 a fringing beach e.g. at the strandline of a sandy beach
  2 a shingle bar crossing a bay e.g. Chesil Beach in Dorset, England
  3 a curved spit, the end of which may change as more material collects
  4 forelands, which continue to build new tracts of land e.g. Dungeness in England
- in all cases the build up of shingle comes from long-shore drift: material moves along the coast by the oblique action of waves

PROBLEMS and FEATURES OF SHINGLE

- it is unstable and mobile
- it is often the suddenness of a storm which creates a bank of shingle and just as suddenly breaches it

- there is rapid drainage due to the large spaces between the pebbles; this leads to a poor nutrient state as well as freshwater deficiency
- seawater can percolate through, increasing salinity
- behind the shingle low ground will tend to be saline and brackish lakes may form
- behind the spits salt-marshes develop, the communities merge into the shingle species
- only sheltered, stable areas of shingle become colonised and then only by a very limited group of species

POINTS OF SPECIAL INTEREST

- colonisation and succession can be followed in a similar way to that on sand dunes except the number of species is far less
- it presents a chance to see plants adapted to extreme stress

PRECAUTIONS

- care must be taken since shingle beaches can be steep, unstable and liable to collapse; swimming can be very dangerous due to long-shore currents

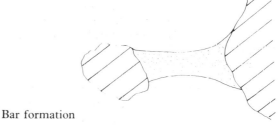

Spit formation

Bar formation

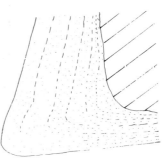

Shingle foreland

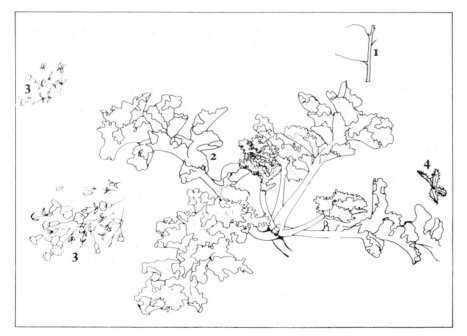

1 *Rumex crispus* (curled dock), dead

2 *Crambe maritima* (sea kale)

3 *Silene maritima* (sea campion)

4 *Silybum marianum* (milk thistle)

- mobile shingle; heavy pebbles will crush organisms
- rapid drainage produces low water and mineral content
- large air spaces
- saline conditions
- localised conditions determine the principle plant species

PIONEER SPECIES

Crambe maritima — (sea kale)
- a member of the cabbage family
- a tough looking perennial; thickened stem bases and woody roots withstand the pressure of the moving shingle
- the leaves are fleshy with a crinkled edge; young leaves are purplish; succulent leaves help to conserve water
- it is the first vascular plant to colonise shingle; nutrients are obtained by an extensive root system and from washed-in seaweeds that have decayed
- the fruits are corky, floating in their dead flower heads, to be dispersed by the sea

Silene maritima — (sea campion) up to 20 cm in height with white flowers
- it is tolerant of well drained areas: found on cliff tops
- it is particularly abundant where nitrogen content has been increased by organic matter deposited on the strandline
- it has deep probing roots
- the plants spread out and collapse across the surface: this reduces water loss and has the effect of stabilising the surface shingle
- humus collects below the prostrate bush and forms the beginnings of soil which encourages sea plantain, cat's ear and others to grow upon it

Silybum marianum — (milk thistle)
- it has white veins and yellow tips to its spines
- it grows as a rosette on shingle, helping to reduce water loss
- it has a deep tap root

ADDITIONAL PLANTS OF SHINGLE

Suaeda vera — (shrubby seablite) 1–1.5 m tall, see also page 72
- it is common in the east of England, where dense bands form just behind the shingle ridges
- as an early pioneer it easily becomes swamped by mobile pebbles and is pushed flat; woody stems survive the weight and produce new stems and roots from this prostrate branch; repetition of this gradually spreads the plant across the shingle, forming the bands and humus (soil) as it goes
- the seeds are dispersed by the sea and they grow deep tap roots on germination

Glaucium flavum — (yellow horned poppy)
- it is semi succulent with leaves close to the shingle
- the large yellow flowers produce long curved seed pods with thousands of tiny black seeds

Lichens
- several species of lichen encrust the larger stones e.g. *Verrucaria maura* (page 13) and *Placodium* species

STABILISED SHINGLE COMMUNITY

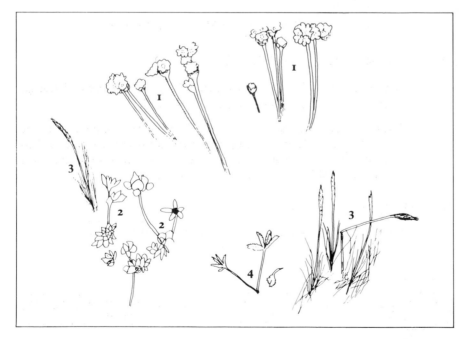

1 *Armeria maritima* (thrift)

2 *Lotus corniculatus* (bird's-foot trefoil)

3 *Festuca rubra* (red fescue)

4 *Ranunculus repens* (creeping buttercup)

• plant cover stabilises the shingle surface, there is minimal
movement
• water and mineral content is low
• less saline than the previous community

Armeria maritima	(thrift or sea-pink, see page 60)

• it is related to the sea-campion (early coloniser) and is also a
cliff species able to tolerate salt spray and dry conditions

Lotus corniculatus   (birdsfoot trefoil, see page 85)

• a common species colonising the areas of sea campion and
replacing it; in the photograph the trefoil has made a
dominant covering of the shingle
• the root nodules fix nitrogen as nitrates, subsequent
enrichment of the soil is important for other plant species;
thus it is an essential part of the early communities

Festuca rubra   (red or creeping fescue, see page 81)

• it is often one of the first grasses to establish itself in a
community
• the rhizomes rapidly colonise an area once established
• the leaves are very narrow and the reduced surface area helps
to conserve water
• a common species of salt-marsh and sand dunes
• the seed-bearing spike is tall so that it can reach air currents
• grazing encourages the grasses and so will eventually result in
shingle pasture

Ranunculus repens   (creeping buttercup)

• a casual visitor from more productive grassland

ADDITIONAL SPECIES OF STABLE SHINGLE

Honkenya peploides   (sea-sandwort) a low, creeping perennial of sand dune and shingle
• its dense leaf arrangement reduces water loss

Nesting birds   Although few feed here, several waders do nest. Chicks are well
camouflaged, such as the ringed plover and oyster-catcher and by
lying still they merge with the shingle. Black headed gulls and terns
use secluded shingle banks for their colonies.

Fig. 21   Summary of colonisation and succession of shingle

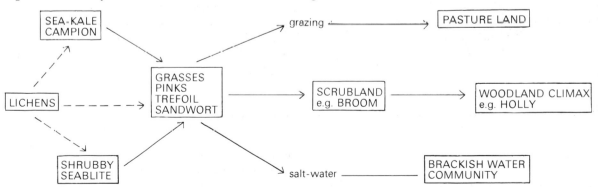

On shingle bars it is not always possible to see the climax community
as they are too narrow and unstable. When broom grows, like other
heathers, it dies from the centre; this allows colonisation by trees.
See the section on succession, pages 88–89.

GLOSSARY

alternation of generation occurrence during the life cycle of seaweeds of different forms from asexual to sexual in seaweeds

annual plant the life cycle is completed in one year; it overwinters as seed

biennial plant the life cycle is completed in two years, flowering in the second year

biomass the total weight of an organism or community (cf. productivity)

climax plant community a community that remains more or less unchanged over a long period of time and is the end result of succession under natural conditions

colonisation the process of animals and plants becoming established in a habitat

conceptacle (re. algae) depressions in the frond where gametes are produced

decomposition the separation and breakdown of cells into an unrecognisable form

detritus microscopic fragments of organic matter

ecdysis the process of shedding the exoskeleton in arthropods e.g. crab

epiphyte a plant using another organism as substrate for attachment (not a parasite)

epizoite an animal living on another organism but not a parasite, e.g. a barnacle attached to a crab's carapace

halophyte a plant able to grow in saline soil

lethal limit the limit of environmental stress (e.g. temperature) that an organism can tolerate, at and beyond which the organism will die

light compensation point the light intensity at which the photosynthesis and respiration in a plant balance each other so there is no net exchange of carbon dioxide and oxygen

limiting factors (abiota) the physical and chemical features of the environment e.g. temperature, light; they affect an organism's survival and distribution

littoral living on the seashore; as a region, it is between high and low tides

machair a type of dune pasture land, usually of a highly calcareous soil, which develops in humid and windy conditions; typical of north-west Scotland

meiofauna microscopic animals which live between wet grains of sediment e.g. sand

metamorphosis a change in form during the life cycle from embryo to adult

microcommunity a community which is usually of a limited diversity of species

microhabitat a small area in the main habitat within which lives a microcommunity

nematocyst sting cells of coelenterates e.g. anemones and hydroids

node the point on a plant stem from where the leaves grow, the *internode* is the space between successive nodes

solute potential the capacity of a solution to absorb water through a partially permeable membrane
N.B. The effect of increasing solute concentration of a solution is to make the osmotic potential of the solution more negative i.e. to *lower* the osmotic potential. A concentrated salt solution thus has a *lower* osmotic potential than a dilute salt solution. An alternative term for osmotic potential is solute potential, Ψ_s.

perennial a plant that continues to grow from year to year

prehensile an adaptation for gripping and holding

productivity the rate at which organic matter is created by photosynthesis

radula a membranous strip with rows of chitinous teeth used in feeding; a characteristic of gastropod molluscs

rhizome a horizontal stem growing under the soil, sending shoots up and roots down

runner a horizontal stem growing above the ground, rooting at nodes

sere communities in succession e.g. one originating from sand dunes is called a xerosere, one originating from rock is a lithosere

siphon (re. molluscs) two muscular tubes which enable bivalves to obtain oxygenated water and food from the surface (inhalent siphon) and deposit waste (exhalent siphon)

standing crop the amount of organic matter in a given area at a specific time; this is likely to change with the season

strandline a line visible above the high tide mark where organic and human flotsam becomes stranded

succession a sequence of communities which develop over a period of time; see SERE

taxis the locomotional response of an organism to a stimulus e.g. sea slaters move away from light

thallus a simple plant body with no differentiation into roots or stem e.g. alga

tidal range the distance the tide rises and falls

transect a series of samples taken at set intervals along a line across a habitat; a *belt transect* is where the results are expressed as a map distribution pattern; a *profile transect* measures the change in height across the habitat

transpiration the loss of water by evaporation from plants, usually from leaves

trophic level a particular stage in a food web through which there is transfer of energy; the stages can be related to nutrition, e.g. autotrophic nutrition

xerophyte a plant able to grow in very dry soil

HINTS FOR ANSWERING THE PROBLEMS

This is intended as a guide to the more difficult questions only.

Rocky shore problems (p. 37)

1a The mean ratios are A 1:2.6 and B 1:36

1b Squat-shaped dog-whelks offer less resistance to wave action. The wider the diameter of the operculum the larger the foot is likely to be for attaching the animal to the substrate (important in turbulent water).

1c Sheltered shores are more likely to have predatory animals such as large crabs (e.g. *Carcinus maenas*).

2b Barnacles are a prominent aspect of the diet throughout the year and are always available on rocks. The jaws of the blenny are large and powerful. Crustaceans are abundant on the shore in summer months.

2c Seven crabs were found in the gut of this blenny.

2d Fly maggots eat dead and decaying seaweed. During the autumn and winter seaweed is washed up on the beach after heavy storms.

2e Guarding eggs provides little time for hunting and adults occasionally eat their eggs.

2f The algae reach extremely high levels in the gut in May.

2g During winter there are fewer potential prey species on the shore; in spring there is often less time to feed as courtship and selection of spawning sites takes priority; after the breeding season the blenny replenishes its fat reserves.

3a Upper shore $\bar{x} = 83.8$ mm, $s = 6.5$; middle shore $\bar{x} = 79.6$ mm, $s = 7.5$; lower shore $\bar{x} = 59.7$ mm, $s = 5.8$

3b Limpets on the upper shore have the shortest time to feed whilst the lower shore has the longest; a long radula can remove more algae from the rock than a shorter one.

4a The densities are: Plot 1 1652; Plot 2 350; Plot 3 2667; Plot 4 362.

4b A high density can only be maintained if there is sufficient food available; productivity of the algae increases with moisture. Populations are affected by predation and disease.

4c Marking with paint could attract the attention of either predators or students. The paint might rub off.

4d Small periwinkles are easily overlooked when collecting the samples.

Sand and mud problems (p. 55)

1b Human haemoglobin produces a sigmoid-shaped dissociation curve and reaches almost 100%.

1c The curve for lugworm is steeper, i.e. the haemoglobin saturates at a low oxygen tension.

1d The blood becomes saturated at different pH values; carbon dioxide is an acidic gas.

1e Oxygen will be transferred from coelomic to vascular haemoglobin; it is possible that the coelomic haemoglobin is used as an oxygen store.

1f Lugworms are found in sand; sand on the upper shore has air spaces, this allows the worm to ventilate atmospheric air; the blood of the lugworm can reach 90% saturation which is higher than the catworm.

2a Both can live side by side with a minimum of competition as *Corophium* ingests fine particles whilst *Hydrobia* consumes larger material.

2b The density of diatoms correlates with the density of *Hydrobia*; the *Corophium* feeds on the smaller bacteria.

2c The size of particle ingested is very specific to a size of *Hydrobia*, a partitioning of the food occurs and the available food is shared between the organisms.

Salt-marsh problems (p. 74)

1a The salt content of the sediment increases towards the lower areas of the salt-marsh; the sap S.P. correlates with the zonation on the salt-marsh so that colonisers such as cord grass have the highest, orache the least.

1b The higher the chloride ion level in the sap the greater the movement of water from the saline sediment into the plant. Sodium chloride is actively taken up from the sediment and one would expect under those conditions that the S.P. would be proportional to the chloride ion present; the seablite figures do not follow this and may help to explain its presence higher up the shore.

2a Early colonisers must be able to tolerate saline conditions; as succession occurs salt is gradually removed by the communities present, thus decreasing the salt content of the sediment; most seem to germinate best in freshwater.

2b Waterlogging will eliminate oxygen, well-established plants will shade young seedlings.

2c It will develop a root system quickly, stabilising the surface.

Sand dune problem (p. 90)

1b Cockchafers, ground beetles and millipedes emerge at night; wolf spiders emerge by day.

1c Snails are active when humidity is high, emerging to feed after rain.

1d Warmth of a mammal (such as a passing rabbit) is the stimulus.

1e Trapping is gradually depleting the population.

REFERENCES

V. J. Chapman, *Coastal Vegetation* (Oxford, Pergamon Press, 1976) tables 5.2 and 5.3

Dowdeswell and Sinker, 1977, *The Study of Ecology*, slides and tape (London, Audio Learning)

J. Green, *The Biology of Estuarine Animals* (London, Sidgwick and Jackson, 1968)

J. D. Jones, 'Observations on the respiratory physiology and on the polychaete genus *Nepthys*', *Journal of Experimental Biology*, **32** (Oxford University Press, 1954)

Prosser and Brown, *Comparative Animal Physiology*, 2nd edn (Philadelphia, W. B. Saunders Co., 1961)

S. Z. Qasim, 'The biology of *Blennius pholis*', *Proceedings of the Zoological Society of London*, **128** (Zoological Society of London, 1957) p. 197

USEFUL IDENTIFICATION KEYS

A field guide to the British brown seaweeds, S. Hiscock (London, Field Studies Council, 1979)

A field guide to the British red seaweeds, S. Hiscock (London, Field Studies Council, 1986)

Animals and plants of the rocky shore, M. Quigley and R. Crump (Oxford, Basil Blackwell, 1986)

Plant computer keys: rocky shores, R. Pankhurst (Cambridge, Cambridge University Press in collaboration with the British Museum of Natural History, 1989)

Seashore studies, M. Jenkins (London, Allen and Unwin, 1983)

Synopses of the British fauna, a series containing detailed keys (London, Academic Press, 1980)

SPECIES INDEX

For ease of use the species have been listed in order of common names where possible; the scientific name has been used where there is no English name. Group names, e.g. sea birds, are also used.

alder (*Alnus glutinosa*) 86–87
amphibians 87
amphipoda 15, 49, 51, 52, 53
Amphitrite johnstoni 42–43
anemone, 1, 16–18, 20, 21, 30, 32, 33, 44–45
   beadlet (*Actinia equina*) 16–18
   gem (*Bunodactis verrucosa*) 21
   snakeslock (*Anemonia viridis*) 18
aphid 59, 61

bacteria 4, 41, 49, 50, 53, 73
baltic tellin (*Macoma*) 47
banded snail (*Lepaea nemoralis*) 80, 83
barnacle 3, 13, 14, 30, 31, 32, 33, 34
beetles 59, 61, 83
bladder-wrack (*Fucus vesiculosus*) 3, 7, 14, 16–18, 28, 30, 31
blenny (*Blennius pholis*) 23, 32, 33, 38
blue-rayed limpet (*Patina pellucida*) 26, 27
bog moss (*Sphagnum*) 86–87
bog myrtle (*Myrica gale*) 86–87
Bostrychia scorpioides 63
bracken (*Pteridium aquilinum*) 83
bristletail (*Petrobius maritimus*) 15
brittle stars 27, 33, 45
buttercup, creeping (*Ranunculus repens*) 94–95

Caloplaca marina 8–9
Calothrix 63
cat's ear (*Hypochaeris radicata*) 6, 76, 79, 80
centipedes 11
Ceramium rubrum 19, 36, 40
channel wrack (*Pelvetia canaliculata*) 12, 13, 14, 28, 29, 30, 36
Chondrus crispus 26, 29, 33
cinnabar moth 81
Cladophora rupestris 18, 20, 35
cockle shell (*Cerastoderma edule*) 42–43, 51, 53
Codium tomentosum 22
common reed (*Phragmites communis*) 46, 59, 60, 68, 72, 74, 87
copepods 48, 65
Corallina officinalis 20–22, 27, 30, 31, 34, 40
cord grass (*Spartina*) 57, 62, 66–68, 69, 70, 71, 72, 73, 74
cormorant 10
Corophium volutator 46, 47, 52, 54, 55, 61
crabs 16–18, 20, 26, 32, 33, 36, 40, 44–45, 48, 53
curlew 54

dabberlocks (*Alaria esculenta*) 31
daisy (*Bellis perennis*) 84–85
daisy anemone (*Cereus pedunculatus*) 44–45
diatoms 48, 49, 53, 56, 73
dock, curled (*Rumex crispus*) 92
dog whelk 3, 19, 30, 32, 33, 37
dulse (*Rhodymenia pseudopalmata*) 25, 26, 35

eel (*Anguilla anguilla*) 65
eel grass (*Zostera*) 45, 57, 69, 72
eider (duck) 19, 54
Enteromorpha intestinalis 15, 29, 34, 46, 48, 53, 57, 60, 67, 69
Eurydice pulchra 42–43

fescue grass 6, 10, 63, 72, 76, 79, 80–81, 94–95
flatworms 65
flounder (*Platichthys flesus*) 49, 65
fox moth (*Macrothylacia rubi*) 83
fulmar 10
furbellows (*Saccorhiza bulbosa*) 26, 32

Gammarus 61, 65
garden snail (*Helix aspersa*) 76–77, 80, 84
Gigartina stellata 26
glasswort (*Salicornia*) 57, 66–67, 70, 71, 72, 73, 74
godwit 54
goose, Brent 69
   grey lag 69
gorse (*Ulex*) 83
greenshank 65
guillemot 10
gull, herring 10, 65

Haustorius arenarius 45

heather, bell (*Erica cinerea*) 83
   cross-leaved (*Erica tetralix*) 87
heron 54
horned wrack (*Fucus ceranoides*) 47, 48
horsetail, water (*Equisetum fluviatile*) 86
hydroids 23

insects 11, 15, 73, 79, 87, 90
iris, yellow (*Iris pseudacorus*) 86–87

kittiwake 10
knot 54
knotted wrack (*Ascophyllum nodosum*) 3, 16–18, 28, 30, 31, 35, 40

Laminaria species 7, 22, 24, 25, 26, 28, 29, 30, 31, 32, 35, 36, 40
Lasaea rubra 15
Laurencia pinnatifida 21, 29
laver spire shell (*Hydrobia ulvae*) 46, 47, 49, 52, 53, 54, 55, 73
Lecanora atra 8–9
lichen 6, 8–9, 11, 12, 13, 14, 15, 16, 17, 30, 31
limpets (*Patella*) 7, 14, 16, 19, 20, 21, 30, 31, 32, 34, 36, 39
Lineus ruber 49
ling (*Calluna vulgaris*) 6, 82–83, 88, 89
Lithophyllum 20, 36
Lithothamnion 22, 30, 31, 34, 35
lugworm (*Arenicola marina*) 42–43, 51, 53, 55
lyme grass (*Elymus arenaria*) 72, 78, 88

mallard 65
marram grass (*Ammophila arenaria*) 6, 75, 76–77, 78, 79, 80–81, 82, 83, 88, 89
marsh pennywort (*Hydrocotyle vulgaris*) 84
masked crab (*Corystes cassivelaunus*) 44, 45
mites 65
mosquito 69, 87
mosses 6, 81, 82–83
mouse-eared chickweed (*Cerastium*) 80–81
mussel (*Mytilus edulis*) 19, 29, 32, 33, 54

Nemalion 36
nematodes 48, 53, 65

Ochrolechia parella 8–9
opossum shrimp (*Neomysis*) 49
orache (*Atriplex hastata*) 59, 74
Orchestia gammarella 15
oystercatcher 3, 19, 23, 54, 95
oysters 49, 54

paddle worms 27
peppery furrow shell (*Scrobicularia plana*) 46, 47, 52, 54
periwinkle 11, 12, 13, 14, 16–18, 28, 29, 32, 33, 73
   black (*Littorina obtusata*) 11
   edible (*L. littorea*) 18, 28
   flat (*L. littoralis*) 16–18, 20, 28
   rough (*L. rudis*) 12, 13, 14, 28, 39
Philaenus spumarius 69
plantain, buckshorn (*Plantago coronopus*) 85
   sea (*Plantago maritima*) 10, 11, 57, 58, 72
plover, ringed 54, 95
Polysiphonia fastigiata 18
Pomatoceros triqueter 23
poppy, yellow horned (*Glaucium flavum*) 93
Porphyra umbilicalis 15
Prasiola stipitata 11
prawn 36
prickly saltwort (*Salsola kali*) 78
protozoa 4, 48, 53, 65
purple moor grass (*Molinia caerulea*) 86–87

rabbit 10, 73, 75, 78, 79, 82, 83, 87
ragworm (*Nereis diversicolor*) 46, 47, 51, 52, 53, 54
ragwort (*Senecio jacobaea*) 80–81
Ramalina siliquosa 8–9
razor shell (*Ensis ensis*) 45
redshank 54, 61, 65
rush 57, 58, 60, 70, 72

salt-marsh bug (*Saldula palustris*) 61
salt-marsh grass (*Puccinellia maritima*) 62–63, 69, 72
sand couch grass (*Agropyron junceiforme*) 3, 72, 78, 88
sand dunes 82–83
sand gaper (*Mya arenaria*) 49, 51, 53, 54
sand goby (*Gobius minutus*) 65

SUBJECT INDEX